Irony

Irony is an intriguing topic, central to the study of meaning in language. This book provides an introduction to the pragmatics of irony. It surveys key work carried out on irony in a range of disciplines such as semantics, pragmatics, philosophy and literary studies, and from a variety of theoretical perspectives including Grice's approach, Sperber and Wilson's echoic account, and Clark and Gerrig's pretence theory. It looks at a number of uses of irony and explores how irony can be misunderstood cross-culturally, before delving into the key debates on the pragmatics of irony: is irony always negative? Why do speakers communicate via irony, and which strategies do they usually employ? How are irony and sarcasm different? Is irony always funny? To answer these questions, basic pragmatic notions are introduced and explained. The book includes multiple examples and activities to enable readers to apply the theoretical frameworks to actual everyday instances of irony.

JOANA GARMENDIA is an assistant professor in the Department of Basque Language and Communication at the University of the Basque Country. She is the assistant secretary of the journal *GOGOA* – the Institute for Logic, Cognition, Language and Information (ILCLI) journal, which is devoted to the study of language, knowledge, communication and action – and a member of the research group 'Language, Action, and Thought' of the ILCLI.

KEY TOPICS IN SEMANTICS AND PRAGMATICS

Key Topics in Semantics and Pragmatics focuses on the main topics of study in semantics and pragmatics today. It consists of accessible yet challenging accounts of the most important issues, concepts and phenomena to consider when examining meaning in language. Some topics have been the subject of semantic and pragmatic study for many years and are re-examined in this series in light of new developments in the field; others are issues of growing importance that have not so far been given a sustained treatment. Written by leading experts and designed to bridge the gap between textbooks and primary literature, the books in this series can either be used on courses and seminars or as one-stop, succinct guides to a particular topic for individual students and researchers. Each book includes useful suggestions for further reading, discussion questions and a helpful glossary.

Already Published in the Series

Meaning and Humour by Andrew Goatly

Metaphor by L. David Ritchie

Imperatives by Mark Jary and Mikhail Kissine

Modification by Marcin Morzycki

Semantics for Counting and Measuring by Susan Rothstein

Forthcoming Titles

Game-Theoretic Pragmatics by Anton Benz

Pragmatics and the Philosophy of Language by Mitchell Green

Distributivity by George Tsoulas and Eytan Zweig

Implicature by Jacques Moeschler and Sandrine Zufferey

Experimental Pragmatics by Ira Noveck

Semantics and Pragmatics in Sign Languages by Kathryn Davidson

Propositional Logic by Allen Hazen and Jeffrey Pelletier

Irony

JOANA GARMENDIA

University of the Basque Country

CAMBRIDGE
UNIVERSITY PRESS

University Printing House, Cambridge CB2 8BS, United Kingdom

One Liberty Plaza, 20th Floor, New York, NY 10006, USA

477 Williamstown Road, Port Melbourne, VIC 3207, Australia

314-321, 3rd Floor, Plot 3, Splendor Forum, Jasola District Centre, New Delhi - 110025, India

79 Anson Road, #06-04/06, Singapore 079906

Cambridge University Press is part of the University of Cambridge.

It furthers the University's mission by disseminating knowledge in the pursuit of
education, learning and research at the highest international levels of excellence.

www.cambridge.org
Information on this title: www.cambridge.org/9781107465916
DOI: 10.1017/9781316136218

© Joana Garmendia 2018

This publication is in copyright. Subject to statutory exception
and to the provisions of relevant collective licensing agreements,
no reproduction of any part may take place without the written
permission of Cambridge University Press.

First published 2018
First paperback edition 2020

A catalogue record for this publication is available from the British Library

Library of Congress Cataloging in Publication data
Names: Garmendia, Joana, 1978– author.
Title: Irony / Joana Garmendia.
Description: Cambridge, U.K. ; New York : Cambridge University Press, [2018] |
Series: Key topics in semantics and pragmatics
Identifiers: LCCN 2017053335 | ISBN 9781107092631 (hardback)
Subjects: LCSH: Irony. | Wit and humor. | Semantics – Research. | Pragmatics – Research.
Classification: LCC P301.5.I73 G27 2018 | DDC 809/.918–dc23
LC record available at https://lccn.loc.gov/2017053335

ISBN 978-1-107-09263-1 Hardback
ISBN 978-1-107-46591-6 Paperback

Cambridge University Press has no responsibility for the persistence or
accuracy of URLs for external or third-party internet websites referred to in
this publication, and does not guarantee that any content on such websites is,
or will remain, accurate or appropriate.

Amari, aitari.
Eta datorrenari.

Contents

List of Figures   page xi
Acknowledgements   xii

1   Introduction   *1*
   1.1 Types of Irony   *3*
       1.1.1 Situational Irony   *3*
       1.1.2 Dramatic Irony   *6*
       1.1.3 Verbal Irony   *7*
   1.2 Irony's Siblings   *9*
   1.3 Irony and Rhetoric   *11*
   1.4 Irony and Pragmatics   *13*
   1.5 Suggested Reading   *16*
       1.5.1 Overviews on Irony   *16*
       1.5.2 Situational Irony   *16*
       1.5.3 Pragmatics   *16*

2   Irony as Opposition   *17*
   2.1 Grice   *18*
   2.2 Problems   *25*
       2.2.1 To Make as if to Say   *26*
       2.2.2 Irony with No Flouting   *27*
       2.2.3 Non-Declarative Irony   *28*
       2.2.4 The Point of Irony   *29*
   2.3 Some Developments   *31*
       2.3.1 Speech Act Theory   *31*
       2.3.2 The *Asif*-Theory   *33*
       2.3.3 Irony as Indirect Negation   *38*

vii

viii   *Contents*

2.4 Summary   *39*

2.5 Suggested Reading   *40*
   2.5.1 Grice   *40*
   2.5.2 Grice's Problems   *40*
   2.5.3 Some Developments   *41*

3   Irony as Echo   *42*

3.1 The Echoic Account   *42*

3.2 Problems   *53*
   3.2.1 Echo   *54*
   3.2.2 Dissociation   *57*

3.3 Some Developments   *59*
   3.3.1 Echoic Reminder Theory   *59*
   3.3.2 Curcó's Proposal   *61*

3.4 Summary   *63*

3.5 Suggested Reading   *63*
   3.5.1 Sperber and Wilson   *63*
   3.5.2 Criticisms of the Echoic Account   *64*
   3.5.3 Some Developments   *64*

4   Irony as Pretence   *65*

4.1 The Pretence Theory   *65*

4.2 Problems   *71*

4.3 Pretence versus Echo   *73*
   4.3.1 In Favour of Pretence   *74*
   4.3.2 In Favour of Echo   *75*
   4.3.3 Types of Irony   *78*
   4.3.4 Types of Victims   *78*
   4.3.5 The Speaker's Tone of Voice   *79*

4.4 Some Developments   *79*
   4.4.1 Walton, Recanati and Currie   *79*
   4.4.2 The Allusional Pretence Theory   *84*

4.5 Summary   *86*

4.6 Suggested Reading   *86*
   4.6.1 Clark and Gerrig's Pretence Theory   *86*
   4.6.2 Criticisms of the Pretence Theory   *87*
   4.6.3 Some Developments   *87*

Contents   ix

5   Attitude Expression in Irony *88*
     5.1 Irony Is Sometimes Positive: The Asymmetry Issue *91*
     5.2 Irony Is Always Negative *95*
          5.2.1 False Positives *96*
          5.2.2 Controversial Cases *100*
     5.3 The Tinge Hypothesis *104*
     5.4 Suggested Reading *105*
          5.4.1 The Attitude in Irony *105*
          5.4.2 Irony Is Negative *106*
          5.4.3 The Tinge Hypothesis *106*
6   Clues of Irony *107*
     6.1 The Risks of Irony *107*
     6.2 Traditional Clues *112*
     6.3 Opposition, Echo and Pretence *114*
          6.3.1 Opposition *115*
          6.3.2 Echo *117*
          6.3.3 Pretence *118*
     6.4 A Minimal Account of Irony *119*
     6.5 Suggested Reading *124*
          6.5.1 Risks and Benefits of Irony *124*
          6.5.2 Traditional Clues *124*
          6.5.3 A Minimal Account of Irony *125*
7   Sarcasm and Humour *126*
     7.1 Irony and Sarcasm *127*
          7.1.1 Victims *130*
          7.1.2 Aggressiveness *133*
          7.1.3 Clarity *134*
          7.1.4 Summary *136*
     7.2 Irony and Humour *138*
          7.2.1 Superiority Theories of Humour *138*
          7.2.2 Incongruity Theories of Humour *141*
          7.2.3 Summary *144*

7.3 Suggested Reading   145

    7.3.1 Sarcasm   145

    7.3.2 Humour   145

Examples Used in Text   147
Glossary   154
Bibliography   157
Index   164

Figures

2.1 Grice's classification of implicatures *page 21*
3.1 Relevance theory: language uses 45

Acknowledgements

Writing this book has been a beautiful challenge. I could not have enjoyed it without the help and encouragement of my family, friends and colleagues. I am in debt to all of them for their understanding and support. *Eskerrik asko denoi.*

I am indebted to my colleagues at the Institute for Logic, Cognition, Language and Information (ILCLI) and to the members of our research group Language, Action, and Thought for useful feedback and encouraging discussions, and especially to Yolanda García Lorenzo, Ekain Garmendia, Kepa Korta and Larraitz Zubeldia, who generously read previous versions of this work and made useful suggestions.

I am grateful to Helen Barton, my editor at Cambridge University Press, for her support and efficiency. And I thank the editorial assistant and content and project managers at Cambridge for their help, as well as the anonymous referees for their comments and suggestions.

This work has been supported in part by the Basque Government (IT1032-16) and the Spanish Ministry of Economy and Competitivity (FFI2015-63719-P, MINECO/FEDER).

1 Introduction

We all know what irony is, or we believe that we do. We say that this or that is ironic, that someone behaves ironically, or that it was ironic that such and such occurred in the way it did. The term appears in everyday conversations as well as in highly specialized theoretical discussions. Its roots originate from the ancient Greek era and have spread and changed over time. Irony is analyzed in many different fields, and very diverse instances are called 'ironic'.

However, the notion of irony is difficult to pinpoint precisely. We use it to characterize diverse elements, and this complicates our efforts to determine the cohesive features of such a varied set. Let us start by considering five separate real-world instances that could easily be called ironic. Observing their similarities and differences will help us assess the complexities of the work we aim to undertake.

Turkish Gay Parade

On 28 June 2015, the annual gay pride parade was held in Istanbul, Turkey. The Turkish police attempted to disperse the crowd using, among other strategies, water cannons. Many attendees were injured by these cannons, but the water also created a rainbow in the sunlight – the symbol of the LGBT pride movement. Someone took a picture of the scene and shared it on the Internet, with the title, 'Police react with water cannons. Karma reacts with rainbow'. The picture was celebrated worldwide.

A Modest Proposal

In 1729, Jonathan Swift wrote *A Modest Proposal*. In this essay – whose complete title is 'A Modest Proposal for Preventing the Children of Poor People from Being a Burthen to Their Parents or Country, and for Making Them Beneficial to the Publick' – Swift proposed that, to fix the problem of poverty in Ireland, poor Irish families should sell their children so that rich families could buy these children and eat their delicate flesh. Thus, both hunger and poverty would be resolved. Swift clearly intended to criticize the attitude of the British towards the Irish and that of the rich towards the poor.

The Obamas

On the 21 July 2008 cover of *The New Yorker* magazine, an illustration by Barry Blitt entitled 'The Politics of Fear' showed a caricature of Barack Obama in a turban and his wife dressed in military clothes and holding a machine gun. The scene is set in the Oval Office, where a portrait of Osama bin Laden hangs above a fireplace with a roaring blaze in which an American flag is burning. While the Obama campaign immediately decried the cartoon as tasteless and offensive, the magazine explained that it was a satire of the distortions, misconceptions and prejudices of which the Obamas were victims.

Oedipus

Oedipus Rex is a Greek tragedy written by Sophocles. The main character, Oedipus, abandons his home after an oracle warns him that he will kill his father and marry his mother. In his escape, he kills a man in a quarrel and marries the Queen of Thebes after solving the riddle of the Sphinx. Oedipus later learns that the man he killed – Laius, King of Thebes – and the woman he married, Jocasta, were his real parents, who abandoned him to die when he was an infant because an oracle had told them that their child would kill his father and marry his mother. However, Oedipus survived and was raised in Corinth, until he escaped to fulfil the fatal destiny he was attempting to escape.

The Big Bang Theory

In the TV series *The Big Bang Theory*, Barry Kripke is the unlikeable colleague of one of the main characters, Leonard Hofstadter. They are both researchers at the California Institute of Technology, and their rivalry is well known to the audience. In episode 13 of season 2, Kripke says to Leonard, 'Heard about your latest anti-proton decay experiment. 20,000 data runs and no statistically significant results. Very impressive', humiliating Leonard for his scientific failure.

An event, a book, an illustration, a story and an utterance: all five instances could certainly easily be labelled ironic. The concept of irony is intended to cover all these different uses of the term, but the more the term is used, the vaguer the concept becomes. This is one of life's little ironies.

1.1 Types of Irony 3

In this introductory chapter, my goal is to clearly define our subject of analysis and explain why we should analyze it from a pragmatic standpoint. To start, I will describe the different types of irony.

1.1 TYPES OF IRONY

Irony is a popular topic for pragmatic analysis. It was a key element in classical pragmatic theories, and it remains in vogue. Nevertheless, not all instances that can be labelled ironic are of interest to pragmatics. This field focuses on analyzing verbal communication; therefore, only irony belonging to the communicative spectrum is considered here. This is what we call 'verbal irony'.

Other types of irony include situational irony and dramatic irony. I will start by explaining how these differ from verbal irony and why they will thus not be included among the examples in this book.

1.1.1 Situational Irony

Within the full spectrum of the things and facts called ironic, a first broad distinction can be made: somebody can *do* something ironic, or something ironic can *occur*. Someone can say, draw, write or do something with the intention of being ironic. In contrast, when the Turkish police created a rainbow with their water cannons in their attempt to stop the gay pride parade, it was considered ironic, but the policemen did not intend to be ironic when opening the water cannons – it just happened. This is a clear example of situational irony, or irony of fate.

I will analyze only the first use of the term: our interest, from a pragmatic standpoint, lies primarily in the fact that somebody can communicate something (intended to be) ironic and not in the fact that something ironic can happen.

Many distinctive features have been ascribed to situational irony. My aim here is not to perform an in-depth analysis of situational irony – I will suggest works at the end of the chapter for further reading. However, I will mention that lack of intentionality is a clear distinguishing feature between situational irony and other types of irony, particularly verbal irony. Let me illustrate this claim with several examples.

Example 1 Basque is a minority language. Its survival is endangered and depends on a small group of speakers (approximately 1 million). Every third of December, Basque speakers celebrate Basque Language Day to highlight the need to protect their language. One year, people were using Twitter to manifest their support for the cause, using the hashtag #EuskararenEguna [#BasqueLanguageDay]. Among these messages, there was one that read as follows:

> *Zaindu maite duzun ori! #EuskararenEguna*
> *[Take care of what you love! #BasqueLanguageDay]*

Interpretation 1 It was just another message supporting the work in favour of Basque, only it was misspelt: it should have said *hori* instead of *ori*. When I first read the tweet, I thought it very ironic that someone claiming that her language needed to be protected committed such a blunder – a situational irony, loud and clear.

Interpretation 2 Out of curiosity, I checked who had had the fat thumbs. I discovered that it was a well-known Basque writer, who would scarcely have made such a mistake. It was then that I realized the misspelling was probably purposeful, and the writer was most likely criticizing those people who do not display much interest in the language the rest of the year but, every third of December, proclaim their concern to all and sundry. Beforehand, I had considered ironic the fact that someone had (accidentally) misspelt a certain tweet; now I believed that someone had intended to be ironic on Twitter. The first case would have been a typical instance of situational irony – the latter was a case of verbal irony.

Example 2 The following was graffitied on a wall:

I DON'T BELIEVE IN GLOBAL WARMING

It appears to be a simple statement denouncing the global warming 'conspiracy' theories. However, the lower parts of the words in the second line are submerged in water (presumably, the water of a risen river). How did this happen?

Interpretation 1 It may be that someone made the graffiti truly to declare her indifference to global warming. In that case, the fact that the river covered the graffiti would be a clear case of situational irony, which nobody intended to happen.

1.1 Types of Irony

> **Interpretation 2** In contrast, it may be that someone, genuinely concerned about the ravages of global warming, made the graffiti such that it appeared covered by accident. In that case, the graffiti artist conveyed something ironically, but it is no longer situational irony – and it is the artist's intention to be ironic that makes the difference.[1]

Situational irony is not intentional. It is, rather, an event or occurrence that simply *happens* and that we consider ironic because of the way it occurred. To state this more clearly, situational irony is 'a state of affairs or an event that seems deliberately contrary to what one expects and is often wryly amusing as a result'.[2]

We can find many examples of situational irony, such as a psychic fair that has been cancelled due to unforeseen circumstances or the case of the scientists worried about global warming who went to Antarctica to study the alarming disappearance of ice but had to be rescued because their ship became trapped in ice. The paradigmatic and most familiar example may be that of the fire station burning in flames.

Activity 1.1.1 Situational Irony

We are surrounded by ironic situations. The Internet, for example, is full of them: if you search for the word 'irony', you will obtain thousands of images showing the most diverse situations. Give it a try. Then select several cases and see which elements you can find:

1. Is it an *intentional* occurrence?
2. Does it have a *negative* character?
3. Is it the *opposite* of what might be expected?

---

[1] This graffiti happens to be a work by well-known street artist Banksy (it can be viewed at www.banksy.co.uk/out.asp). It appeared in Regent's Canal in Camden, North London, in 2009. It was painted to coincide with the United Nations Climate Change Conference held in Copenhagen, presumably to criticize the failure to reach an agreement there to mitigate climate change. Similarly, artist Isaac Cordal's installation entitled, *Politicians Discussing Global Warming* (Berlin, 2011), showed a group of men in suits debating something while water reaches up to their necks. The installation is part of the series *Follow the Leaders* and can be viewed at http://cementeclipses.com/Works/follow -the-leaders/ (accessed April 2017).

[2] *Oxford Dictionary of English*: 'irony', second entry; available at https://en.oxford dictionaries.com/definition/irony (accessed April 2017).

6   1 INTRODUCTION

1.1.2 Dramatic Irony

There is a type of irony related to fictional storytelling. Oedipus' story is a classic example: the readers know, while the character does not, that Oedipus himself is the murderer he is seeking. This is an instance of 'dramatic irony': '[a] literary technique, originally used in Greek tragedy, by which the full significance of a character's words or actions is clear to the audience or reader although unknown to the character'.[3]

Ancient Greek dramatists were masters of dramatic irony. The word 'irony' itself derives from these plays: Eiron was one of the main characters of ancient Greek comic plays. He pretended to be a clumsy underdog but ultimately always revealed himself as a witty and clever man, triumphing over Alazon, the overconfident but hopeless character.

We can find many instances of dramatic irony in different literary or artistic trends. Romeo killed himself because he believed Juliet was dead, whereas the reader knows all along that she is not. In the film *The Sixth Sense* (M. Night Shyamalan, 1999), Dr Malcolm Crowe, a child psychologist in Philadelphia, is trying to help nine-year-old Cole Sear, who claims that he can see dead people. At the beginning, Crowe distrusts the boy and doubts that there really are dead people talking to him. However, at the end of the movie, Crowe realizes that he himself was murdered some time ago and has been dead during Cole's entire treatment.

I will not consider this type of ironic instance in this book. I will focus instead on examples of verbal irony because it is these that illustrate the general issue concerning us from a pragmatic standpoint: how it is that someone does (or says) something with the intention to communicate ironically?[4]

Activity 1.1.2   Dramatic Irony

Try to think of examples of dramatic irony in movies, plays or any other type of fictional work.

1. Who is the character in the dark?
2. Do other characters know better? If so, do they realize the irony in it?
3. Does the author share the irony with the audience from the beginning? If not, when and how is it revealed?

---

[3] *Oxford Dictionary of English*: 'irony', third entry; available at https://en.oxford dictionaries.com/definition/irony (accessed April 2017).

[4] Obviously, we can find examples in which someone communicates ironically in fictional works as well, but these would be cases of verbal irony and not of dramatic irony. Dramatic irony applies to the particular use of irony I have described here and not to any instance of irony that occurs within a fictional work.

1.1 Types of Irony

7

> **Other Types of Irony**
>
> **Socratic Irony.** This type of irony, which owes its name to Socrates, consists in feigning ignorance and desire to learn, with the aim of exposing the ignorance of others through their attempt to explain their (erroneous) views.
>
> **Romantic Irony.** This ironic attitude is found in literary works (typically narrative) and commonly refers to authors of the Romantic period who exhibit a certain attitude of scepticism toward their own works, displaying attitudes of self-mockery and a strong awareness of the limitations of their work.

1.1.3 Verbal Irony

Of all the instances that can typically be labelled ironic, only those in the realm of communication concern us here. In all cases, we have a speaker (or writer) who intends to communicate something ironically and an audience who will (or will not) understand what the speaker is communicating. Thus, in this book, I will analyze ironic communication and explain how speakers bring their audiences to understand what they are ironically communicating. I will discuss the ironic speaker's intentions, her tone, her strategies, and the goals pursued when someone decides to express herself ironically.

We might wonder whether someone can communicate something ironically without using language, that is, to what extent must verbal irony be *verbal*. For example, someone can clap when a friend clumsily falls, thus wordlessly expressing ironic disapproval. Let us revisit the episode of *The Big Bang Theory* in which Kripke ironically criticizes Leonard's lack of results in his experiments: he could also do so by giving the thumbs-up instead of uttering, as he did, 'Very impressive!'.

From a pragmatic standpoint, we are interested in analyzing utterances – intentional communicative acts. Acts produced via language are the most typical among these. However, clapping can easily be explained within these parameters as well: when we applaud in a certain context, our act can only be understood as an intentional act of communicating approval. Highly conventionalized acts (such as clapping, giving the thumbs-up or shaking one's head) can be viewed as intentional acts of communication that use no words. Thus, we can pragmatically explain what we communicate when we shake our head negatively. Furthermore, we can also explain how we can communicate something ironic when we clap at a clumsy friend.

Among the cases in which someone is communicating something ironically, I will target those which use language. I am certain our findings will be transferrable to non-linguistic acts of communication: by explaining how someone can be ironic when exclaiming 'Good job!' to somebody who has just broken a delicate and expensive glass vase, we shall surely better understand how someone can be ironic when clapping in the same circumstances.

We thus understand verbal irony as the intentional act of communicating something, typically using language to do so. Another specification is in order here: speakers utter words, sentences, paragraphs or even entire discourses with ironic intent. Sometimes it is simply because a text is filled with ironic utterances that we consider it to be ironic as well; in other cases, we may be convinced of an entire book's ironic nature while being unable to specify any single element in it that is clearly ironic. Jonathan Swift's work serves as a perfect example of the latter, for the entire text should be understood ironically and not as a series of ironic claims.

Activity 1.1.3   Verbal Irony

Think of three examples of verbal irony: cases in which someone intends to communicate something ironically with an utterance. Write them down – they will be useful to you when the time comes to focus on different pragmatic theories of irony. However, let us first verify your intuitions:

1. Are they funny?
2. Do they convey something negative?
3. Do they involve any type of contrast between meanings?

These will be your three irony samples going forward. I will ask you to examine them every time I introduce a new idea about irony.

Discussion

I will provide a sample below to help you with a practical example. This will be the ironic utterance sample that I will use throughout the activities you will encounter in the following chapters:

> Maia and Ku are good friends and know each other well. Ku always rants about women driving terribly, and Maia always argues with him, asserting that it is nonsense to correlate gender and driving ability. One day, they see someone crashing a car into a traffic light. When they approach the car, they see that the driver is a man. Maia exclaims,

> (0) That was a clumsy woman driving.

Irony and Art

It is not uncommon to witness artistic creation described as ironic.

- American artist Andy Warhol's famous *paintings*, for instance, are often considered ironic, such as when he presents products of mass consumption as objects of high art. He played with ambiguity and was thought to be conveying mocking judgement behind the apparent splendour of his paintings. These elements make us associate Warhol's work with an ironic feeling.
- Irony can also be found in *music*. Russian composer Dmitri Shostakovich's music, for example, is considered to be highly ironic in terms of the extent to which extreme contrasts of mood are combined within them, playing with a mocking ambiguity (Elleström 1996).
- We find similar examples in *dance*. American dancer, choreographer and director Mark Morris's choreographies, for instance, have been considered an example of ironic creations, as they shockingly combine different music and dance styles with suggestive gestures (Carroll 2013).

This type of irony is intentional on the part of the creator. Moreover, paintings, music and dance may be considered to be expressing, conveying, meaning or even communicating something. Regardless, that way of meaning or conveying is different from what we call verbal communication and is thus outside the scope of our present study – even if findings in verbal ironic communication may be relevant to the study of these other cases and vice versa.

As I intend to analyze irony from a pragmatic standpoint, among the different levels of linguistic excerpts that I present, I shall focus on analyzing ironic utterances of simple sentences. It goes without saying that I expect our findings to be useful in explaining other levels of verbal irony as well.

1.2 IRONY'S SIBLINGS

Irony is often confused with parody, satire and, in particular, sarcasm. Authors working in the field take different positions regarding this issue, and what certain authors label ironic is considered to be sarcastic or parodic by others.

10   1 INTRODUCTION

> **Definition**
>
> **Parody.** Writing, music, art, speech, etc. that intentionally copies the style of someone famous or copies a particular situation, making the features or qualities of the original more noticeable in a way that is humorous. (*Cambridge Dictionary*)

> **Definition**
>
> **Satire.** A way of criticizing people or ideas in a humorous way, or a piece of writing or play that uses this style. (*Cambridge Dictionary*)

> **Definition**
>
> **Sarcasm.** The use of remarks that clearly mean the opposite of what they say, made in order to hurt someone's feelings or to criticize something in a humorous way. (*Cambridge Dictionary*)

These disagreements point to a certain basic confusion; that is, not only do the theoretical approaches disagree when categorizing these phenomena, but speakers of natural language do not always differentiate among instances of sarcasm, irony and others in the same way either. Differences among cultures appear to play a role here, as different language communities appear to label the same instance of irony, sarcasm and so on differently. For example, a tendency has been noted in recent years in the United States to consider sarcastic what would typically be considered a case of irony in other cultures (and indeed what had been long accepted as ironic in the United States).[5]

However, it appears that borderline cases do exist: cases that are not easily categorized as one thing or another and that appear to be either one or the other depending on the conceptual background from which we examine them.

How should we address this issue? A theory will commonly denounce another for not being able to explain such and such type of case that

---

[5] Geoffrey Nunberg drew our attention to this fact (Nunberg 2001: 91–93). He states: 'For a lot of people now, *sarcasm* is simply a cover term for pointed humor of any kind, from satire and parody to simple banter' (Nunberg 2001: 91). He offers a list of examples that effectively illustrate this change in meanings: 'Wherever you look, irony's moving out and sarcasm's moving in. Johnny Carson was ironic, David Letterman is sarcastic. *Peanuts* was ironic, *South Park* is sarcastic. Andy Warhol was ironic, Jeff Koons is sarcastic. John Waters is ironic, Todd Solondz is sarcastic' (Nunberg 2001: 92).

1.3 Irony and Rhetoric

should be explainable as irony. Similarly, certain theories have been criticized for embracing in their analysis instances of not genuinely ironic cases (and for not being able to differentiate them from authentic irony). It is challenging to take a stance here, as we are attempting to theorize a natural set of cases. A desirable theory may be one that is capable of explaining clear, non-questionable cases of irony, distinguishing them from obvious sarcasm, parodies and other similar phenomena, and clarifying why some cases are arguable or difficult to categorize.

With regard to our present task, I will focus on analyzing clear instances of irony, namely, those which have been considered non-problematic by all theories in the field. Subsequently, we will have the opportunity to examine the relationship between irony and sarcasm (in Section 7.1).

1.3 IRONY AND RHETORIC

Verbal irony has been analyzed in different fields, and different ways of examining verbal irony have resulted in different conceptions of it: is verbal irony a persuasive device, a rhetorical figure or a pattern of communication? This is not a particularity of irony: what to a chemist appears to constitute a set of molecules is a bipedal mammal to a biologist, an intelligent human being to a psychologist and an individual member of society to a sociologist. Indeed, depending on our field, we use different tools to examine the same thing; thus, different features will draw our attention, and the same thing will appear different.

We could approach verbal irony from the perspective of Aristotelian rhetoric, bearing in mind Aristotle's lesson on the persuasive aim of every discourse. Aristotle viewed rhetoric as the faculty of observing in any given case the available means of persuasion, and he distinguished three types of technical means of persuasion: the first is linked to the character of the speaker; the second, to the emotions of the audience; and the third, to the argument itself. It appears that Aristotle would include irony in the first type, as it affects how we perceive the speaker: '[i]rony better befits a gentleman than buffoonery; the ironical man jokes to amuse himself, the buffoon to amuse other people' (Aristotle, Rhetoric, III, 18, 1419b, 7).

Irony has also been viewed as a persuasive device by more recent rhetoricians.[6]

---

[6] However, what Perelman and Olbrechts-Tyteca describe appears closer to Socratic irony.

12   1 INTRODUCTION

> Similarly the most characteristic form of quasi-logical argumentation by the ridiculous consists in temporarily accepting a statement contradictory to that one wishes to defend ... The provisional assumption with which arguments of this sort begin can be expressed in the rhetorical figure of *irony*. (Perelman & Olbrechts-Tyteca 1971: 207)

If we approached irony from this branch of rhetoric, we would explain that Jonathan Swift employed irony to make his works or himself as an author attractive, persuasive and convincing to persuade his audience that something had to be done to address poverty in Ireland.

Rhetoricians also focused on the study of the ornamental aspects of language, as did Quintilian, and as could we: we could embark on our analysis armed with a list of rhetorical figures, and then we would consider irony to be a text-embellishing wink used by the writer to state one thing and mean another – a figure of speech, similar to metaphors, similes and hyperbolae.

Irony could be treated either as a trope or as a figure, according to Quintilian, and in both cases the meaning would be the same: 'Irony involving a *figure* does not differ from the *irony* which is a *trope*, as far as its *genus* is concerned, since in both cases we understand something which is the opposite of what is actually said' (Quintilian, Institutio Oratoria, Book IX, II, 40).

If we viewed irony from this perspective, we would focus on certain literary passages from Swift's *A Modest Proposal* and observe how certain paragraphs, expressions and utterances have been embellished with an ironic twist, such as when he states, 'I can think of no one objection, that will possibly be raised against this proposal, unless it should be urged, that the number of people will be thereby much lessened in the kingdom'.

Different schools of rhetoric focused on different characteristics of verbal irony and thus offered diverse explanations of it. Nevertheless, they all considered irony on a discursive level. Pragmatics, a field that emerged long after rhetoric, analyzes language at a more basic level – utterances are its main focus. The pragmatician aims to explain how language is used in communication. A new way to examine irony arises here. From a pragmatic perspective, we are interested in how a speaker can communicate something with an ironic utterance, why she would decide to be ironic instead of plainly literal, how hearers can grasp the speaker's ironic intentions and so on.

When we approach irony from the perspective of pragmatics, we can explain how someone, following the general rules of conversation, can in fact communicate her disapproval to a friend by uttering 'Good job!' ironically.

1.4 *Irony and Pragmatics* 13

We could start analyzing verbal irony from many points. However, I intend to start our analysis from the very basis: explaining how someone can utter a single sentence to say something ironically. We shall start analyzing utterances, trusting that our findings on this level will help us to better understand verbal irony at different levels.

Pragmatics will be our point of departure. The tools we are using are familiar concepts: we shall identify the speaker's beliefs and intentions, her communicative plan and her utterances' contents, and we shall classify them with propositions. As we approach our goal with all these instruments, irony will appear to us in this way: as a pattern used by speakers to communicate something.

Irony requires a pragmatic clarification for us to start understanding the complex use of the term based on its more basic application.

1.4   IRONY AND PRAGMATICS

Natural language has been analyzed in many fields and, therefore, from distinctly different standpoints. Rhetoric has focused overall on analyzing discourse: how language is used to create persuasive, strong, beautiful texts. Logic and semantics also endeavour to explain language, but on a different level: they both aim to examine types of expressions – sentences. In contrast, pragmatics is often thought to analyze language in context; that is, pragmatics focuses on utterances: concrete events, intentional acts of speakers at specific times and places.

Two different levels of utterance are of interest to pragmatists: first, the aim of pragmatics is to clarify what is *said* by an utterance (what a speaker is actually saying when using a sentence in a specific context); second, pragmatics also intends to explain what a speaker *does* via an utterance, beyond saying.[7]

Irony challenges pragmatics: ironic speakers communicate divergent (or even contradictory) contents compared with the conventional meanings of the uttered sentences or with what one says when uttering a sentence non-ironically – such as when someone utters 'He is a fine friend' regarding a traitor or 'You sure know a lot!' to someone who is arrogantly flaunting his knowledge. Context and common knowledge play a major role in ironic

---

[7] As Korta and Perry stated, this would approximate the difference between nearside and far-side pragmatics (Korta & Perry 2006).

14   1 INTRODUCTION

communication, and these players make irony a tremendously interesting phenomenon from a pragmatic standpoint. Analyzing how speakers communicate with ironic utterances will help us understand how language works.

Most pragmatists have identified this need and have offered many explanations for irony: explanations that are intended to be simple and to catch irony's obvious uniqueness along with sharp explanations meant to fit into precise general theories. My next step in this book will be to examine the three main theoretical trends that aim to explain irony from the pragmatics' perspective: the Gricean account, in Chapter 2; the echoic theory, in Chapter 3; and the pretence theory, in Chapter 4.

The first element that may surprise you is that each theory of irony appears to have a different conception of irony. Paul Grice is a primary proponent of the view of irony as involving an opposition. This has been the classical view of irony from time immemorial, and it unites many authors working on pragmatics in addition to Grice. The view of irony as echo corresponds to another broad general theory of pragmatics – Dan Sperber and Deirdre Wilson's relevance theory – and it also has many adepts. Herbert Clark and Richard Gerrig defend the idea of irony as pretence, among many other authors who have developed this idea in different directions.

I will employ the next three chapters to present the aforementioned theories of irony, explain their strengths and identify their weaknesses. Once we start, we will notice that the differences we detected at first may not be as decisive as anticipated. Although they offer different descriptions of verbal irony, all authors appear to agree on one point: in irony, the speaker does not intend to communicate that which she appears to be putting forward. From this basic point of departure, different theories arise.

There is another point on which everybody working on verbal irony from a pragmatic standpoint appears to agree – the importance of attitude expression in irony. This constitutes another crucial pillar of the analysis of ironic communication, and I will elaborate on it in Chapter 5.

The last two chapters are devoted to more specific aspects of ironic communication. In Chapter 6, I will explain why the way in which speakers communicate ironically is important and introduce the idea of ironic clues – features or means of expressions that speakers use when being ironic. In explaining how we are ironic, we will also touch on the question of why we are ironic.

1.4 Irony and Pragmatics

In Chapter 7, I will broaden the discussion and discuss the relationships between irony and two close phenomena. First, I will attempt to shed light on the distinction between irony and sarcasm. To bring the chapter and the book to a close, I will focus on the links between irony and humour.

A Note on the Examples I Will Use

In the following chapters, I use many ironic examples to illustrate the ideas I am presenting. They are all instances of verbal irony communicated via a single utterance. I will enumerate these ironic utterances with a number in brackets. The example of irony I introduced in Activity 1.1.3 is numbered as utterance **(0)** in my list. You can find the full list of such examples at the end of the book.

The examples in this selection have varied sources. Many already belong to the pragmatic literature on irony – they have been used and analyzed by different authors and theories. A number of these exemplify a particular question relevant to analyzing irony – they were introduced to treat a particular point, and now they almost represent it. I will also use real-world cases as examples, including conversations, dialogues from movies or TV series, pieces of news, literary fragments and so on.

I wish to provide a clarification before we start. We often use irony to mock, ridicule or deride. Sometimes the target of irony is a specific person; other times it is a country, a culture, a category of people or any other identifiable group. In the examples I will use in this book, irony will have diverse types of targets. Moreover, contextual information is important in irony – often it is not easy to understand an ironic utterance if we are not familiar with the details or with the general setting. As I cannot know the context in which the readers of this book are situated, I will attempt to use examples related to globally known topics. We will thus refer to commonly shared stereotypes, social issues such as wars or political conflicts and so on. Consequently, the examples may not always be politically correct, as they may refer to widespread pejorative assumptions. However, this is an academic work, and examples are just that – examples. My aim is to analyze how and why a speaker communicated such and such ironically, without evaluating what it is that this speaker manifested and with no intent to endorse these opinions or claims myself.

1.5 SUGGESTED READING

1.5.1 Overviews on Irony

While the following two works focus mainly on the linguistic manifestation of the phenomenon, they do provide a general overview of the classical conception of irony:

Booth, W. 1974. *A Rhetoric of Irony*. Chicago: University of Chicago Press.
Muecke, D. 1969. *The Compass of Irony*. London: Methuen.

The following is a compilation of some of the most influential articles on irony, which we will assuredly reference repeatedly throughout this book:

Gibbs, R. W. & H. L. Colston (eds.). 2007. *Irony in Language and Thought: A Cognitive Science Reader*. New York: Erlbaum Associates.

1.5.2 Situational Irony

The first article below sheds light on the distinction between verbal and situational irony – or, more generally, between intentional and unintentional irony. The second focuses on the concept of situational irony and provides experimental data on the issue.

Gibbs, R. W. & J. O'Brien. 1991. Psychological aspects of irony understanding. *Journal of Pragmatics* 16: 523–30.
Lucariello, J. 1994. Situational irony: a concept of events gone awry. *Journal of Experimental Psychology: General* 123(2): 129–45.

1.5.3 Pragmatics

For a general introduction to pragmatics, the entry in the *Stanford Encyclopedia of Philosophy* offers a most adequate overview. Levinson's book is a classic introduction to the field, and Horn and Ward's handbook collects papers addressing the fundamental issues in pragmatics.

Horn, L. R. & G. Ward (eds.). 2004. *The Handbook of Pragmatics*. Oxford: Blackwell.
Korta, K. & J. Perry. 2006. Pragmatics. In *The Stanford Encyclopedia of Philosophy*, ed. E. N. Zalta (Winter 2006 edn). Available at http://plato.stanford.edu/archives/spr2007/entries/pragmatics/.
Levinson, S. 1983. *Pragmatics*. New York: Cambridge University Press.

2 Irony as Opposition

Verbal irony has classically been conceived of as the act of saying something and meaning the opposite. That, along with certain other features traditionally associated with irony (such as humour or the expression of an attitude), composes the pre-theoretical conception of irony we typically share:

> The expression of one's meaning by using language that normally signifies the opposite, typically for humorous or emphatic effect.[1]

> The use of words that are the opposite of what you mean, as a way of being funny.[2]

> The use of words that mean the opposite of what you really think especially in order to be funny.[3]

The idea of opposition has also tinged the rhetorical conception of irony:

> Irony's general characteristic is to make something understood by expressing its opposite. (*Encyclopedia of Rhetoric* 404)

While the goal of meaning what one actually believes is repeated in every entry, the definitions are unclear regarding how the speaker achieves this. We are told that the speaker *uses language* that signifies the opposite, *uses words* that are (or mean) the opposite or *expresses* the opposite of what she intends to mean. The attempt to avoid the term included in the classical idea of irony – that the speaker *says* the opposite of what she means – is blatant at this point. Here we can discern the first challenge set by irony: how can it be possible that we mean the opposite of what we say?

---

[1] *Oxford Dictionary of English*, 'irony', first entry, available at https://en.oxforddiction aries.com/definition/irony (accessed April 2017).

[2] *Cambridge Dictionary*, 'irony', second entry, available at http://dictionary .cambridge.org/dictionary/english/irony (accessed April 2017).

[3] *Merriam-Webster Dictionary*, 'irony', second entry, available at www.merriam -webster.com/dictionary/irony (accessed April 2017).

18   2 IRONY AS OPPOSITION

It is at this point that the field of pragmatics is pressed to intervene to clarify how it is that we use words or express something without really saying it. The conception of irony as an opposition had its first pragmatic reconstruction in Grice's account.

2.1 GRICE

Herbert Paul Grice was a pioneer in pragmatics. Grice's pragmatic work focused on explaining the difference between the conventional meanings of words, what the speaker says when uttering them and what she means when doing so.

Speakers commonly communicate things that they do not say. Grice coined the term 'implicature' to explain this fact: what one communicates is typically the sum of what one says and what one implicates. What the speaker says is determined by the conventional meaning of the words she uses (along with a number of pragmatic processes, such as disambiguation and reference fixing). However, there is typically more to natural conversation than what one says: the non-literal meaning communicated by the speaker is explained in terms of implicatures in Grice's theory of conversation.

There are different ways in which a speaker can communicate something without saying it, and thus there are different types of implicatures in Grice's account. Sometimes implicatures are triggered by the conventional meanings of certain words.

(1) He is an Englishman; he is, therefore, brave.

(Grice 1967a/89: 25)

According to Grice, the speaker in **(1)** has said no more than that he is an Englishman and that he is brave (whomever the speaker is referring to by 'he'). Nevertheless, there is something else that the speaker has indicated (and committed herself to its being the case): that his being brave is a consequence of his being an Englishman. This is something that the speaker has communicated without properly saying it – it is an implicature of her utterance. As the implicature in question is determined by the conventional meaning of the word 'therefore', it is an instance of a 'conventional implicature'.[4]

However, when we mention implicatures, we are typically referring to non-conventional implicatures and, in particular, to conversational implicatures, which are essentially connected with certain general

---

[4] Conventional implicatures are among Grice's most controversial contributions. See, for example, Bach (1999) and Karttunen & Peters (1979).

2.1 Grice 19

features of discourse. These implicatures are triggered by contextual and background information, the fact that the speaker has said what she has said and a certain general principle that participants in a conversation, according to Grice, are expected to observe.

Cooperative Principle
Make your conversational contribution such as is required, at the stage at which it occurs, by the accepted purpose or direction of the talk exchange in which you are engaged. (Grice 1967a/89: 26)

Several maxims and sub-maxims accompany this principle in Grice's account.

Quantity
1. Make your contribution as informative as is required (for the current purposes of the exchange).
2. Do not make your contribution more informative than is required.

Quality
Supermaxim: Try to make your contribution one that is true.

1. Do not say what you believe to be false.
2. Do not say that for which you lack adequate evidence.

Relation
Be relevant.

Manner
Supermaxim: Be perspicuous.

1. Avoid obscurity of expression.
2. Avoid ambiguity.
3. Be brief (avoid unnecessary prolixity).
4. Be orderly.[5]

(Grice 1967a/89: 26–27)

Conversational implicatures generally arise when a speaker flouts a maxim (i.e. she blatantly fails to fulfil it). In such cases, Grice states that a maxim has been exploited. The speaker intends the hearer to recognize that she exploited such a maxim and, thus, that she is intending to communicate something else than what she has said – an implicature.

---

[5] Grice later proposed the addition of another maxim of manner:

I would be inclined to suggest that we add to the maxims of Manner which I originally propounded some maxim which would be, as it should be, vague: 'Frame whatever you say in the form most suitable for any reply that would be regarded as appropriate' or 'Facilitate in your form of expression the appropriate reply.' (Grice 1981/89: 273)

20   2 IRONY AS OPPOSITION

This is a general pattern of how a hearer can infer an implicature generated by the exploitation of a maxim:

> He has said that p; there is no reason to suppose that he is not observing the maxims, or at least the CP [cooperative principle]; he could not be doing this unless he thought that q; he knows (and knows that I know that he knows) that I can see that the supposition that he thinks that q is *required*; he has done nothing to stop me thinking that q; he intends me to think, or is at least willing to allow me to think, that q; and so he has implicated that q. (Grice 1967a/89: 31)

There are two types of conversational implicatures according to Grice. In some cases, the use of certain words or expressions will typically (in the absence of special circumstances, he states) carry a certain implicature.

(2) X is meeting a woman this evening.

(Grice 1967a/89: 37)

The speaker in **(2)** can typically be understood to implicate that X is meeting a woman other than his wife, mother, sister, etc. This type of case constitutes what Grice calls 'generalized conversational implicatures' (GCIs).

However, again, there are other types of implicatures as well. Typically, implicatures are generated by the speaker saying something in a particular context and in virtue of certain specific contextual features. These are what Grice names 'particularized conversational implicatures'. Among the latter, the speaker will communicate different types of implicatures depending on the maxims she is flouting.

Instances of figurative meaning are created by flouting the first maxim of quality, 'Do not say what you believe to be false'. These include metaphor, meiosis, hyperbole and the one we are concerned with here, irony.

Grice thus considered irony to be a case of figurative meaning in which the speaker blatantly flouts the maxim of quality and thereby communicates an implicature. What distinguishes irony from other cases of figurative meaning is that the ironic implicature is the contradictory of what the speaker appears to be putting forward.

> X, with whom A has been on close terms until now, has betrayed a secret of A's to a business rival. A and his audience both know this. A says:
>
> (3) X is a fine friend.
>
> (Grice 1967a/89: 34)

2.1 Grice

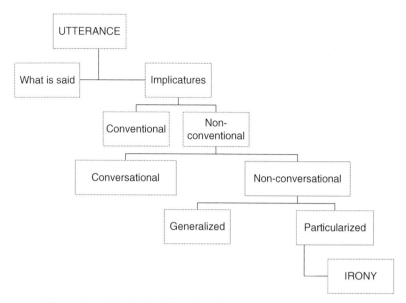

Figure 2.1 Grice's classification of implicatures

This classical Gricean example of irony shows how a speaker can communicate something (that X is not a fine friend) by using a sentence that if uttered in non-ironic circumstances would typically communicate precisely the contradictory (that X is a fine friend). Hearers arrive at what the speaker intends to communicate by recognizing the exploitation of the maxim.

> It is perfectly obvious to A and his audience that what A has said or has made as if to say is something he does not believe, and the audience knows that A knows that this is obvious to the audience. So, unless A's utterance is entirely pointless, A must be trying to get across some other proposition than the one he purports to be putting forward. This must be some obviously related proposition; the most obviously related proposition is the contradictory of the one he purports to be putting forward. (Grice 1967a/89: 34)

In irony, even if the maxim of quality is violated at the level of what is said (or made as if to say), that maxim is observed at the level of what is implicated: the speaker does believe what she implicates to be true. This apparently oblique manner of communicating is secured by the

22　2 IRONY AS OPPOSITION

speaker's *perfectly obvious* flouting of the maxim, along with the fact that what she intends to communicate is *the most obviously related proposition.*

Grice's account is a pragmatic reconstruction of the traditional and pre-theoretical view of irony, in which the speaker is perceived as saying something and meaning the opposite. However, in Grice's account, the speaker is considered to be *making as if to say* the literal meaning of the utterance. What precisely Grice intended to mean with this expression (used again when explaining metaphor) is not entirely clear, but we can venture that he intended to capture the idea repeated in every dictionary entry of irony: *making as if to say* would refer to the act of using words without properly saying them.

Grice may have been attempting to address a problem he faced when explaining irony, a problem we could call 'the contradiction issue': if, according to Grice, what a speaker communicates is the sum of what she says and what she implicates, and we accept that ironic speakers implicate the contradictory of the literal meaning of their utterances, then, assuming that ironic speakers *say* this literal meaning would condemn them to always be communicating a contradiction. Ironic speakers would be committed to a pair of contradictory meanings, as every speaker is committed to both what she says and what she implicates.

To clarify: if we accept that the speaker when uttering **(3)** has said that X is a fine friend, and yet we are willing to claim that she has implicated that X is not a fine friend, we consequently have to accept that the speaker has communicated that X is a fine friend and that X is not a fine friend, namely, a plain contradiction.

This appears to be why Grice holds that speakers, when being ironic, make as if to say the literal meaning of the utterance. Thus we can presume (even if Grice does not openly state so) that by making as if to say a meaning, a speaker can put forward a proposition without committing herself to it. This is how speakers would not be doomed to communicating a contradiction when being ironic.

This is what Grice explained with regard to irony in his seminal work, 'Logic and Conversation' (1967a/89). Aware that his explanations were lacking in several respects, he elaborated on them in 'Further notes on logic and conversation' (1967b/89). There he mentioned three ideas that have subsequently been extensively discussed in the pragmatics of irony.

2.1 Grice

> ### Activity 2.1A   The Gricean View
>
> It is time to test Grice's basic claims on our everyday ironic examples. Take the three samples you selected in Activity 1.1.3 and attempt to answer the following questions. You can view the answers for my sample below.
>
> 1. What is it that the speaker has made as if to say with her ironic utterance? What was she in fact intending to communicate?
> 2. Is the latter contradictory to the former?
> 3. Bearing in mind what you know about implicatures, would you say that what the speaker has communicated is an implicature?
>
> #### Discussion
>
> (0) That was a clumsy woman driving.
>
> 1. Maia has made as if to say that that was a clumsy woman driving, and she has communicated that it was not a clumsy woman driving (but a clumsy man and, probably, that it is nonsense to claim that women drive terribly because they are women).
> 2. *Yes.* There is a contradiction between what she has made as if to say (that it was a clumsy woman driving) and what she has communicated (that it was not a woman driving, among other things).
> 3. *Yes.* It can certainly be considered an implicature, as it is something that the speaker has not said and has communicated by uttering this sentence in this exact context (i.e. the speaker would not necessarily have communicated this if she had uttered the same sentence in another situation).

(i)   Irony Is (Always) Negative

> [I]rony is intimately connected with the expression of a feeling, attitude, or evaluation. I cannot say something ironically unless what I say is intended to reflect a hostile or derogatory judgment or a feeling such as indignation or contempt. (Grice 1967b/89: 53–54)

The first dilemma Grice faced was to pinpoint the missing element of irony that could distinguish real ironic cases from cases in which the speaker puts forward a literal meaning that is obviously the opposite of what she believes but still fail to be actual cases of irony, such as the following:

> A and B are walking down the street, and they both see a car with a shattered window. B says:

24   2 IRONY AS OPPOSITION

(4) Look, that car has all its windows intact.

(Grice 1967b/89: 53)

This utterance cannot be understood as the speaker's attempt to ironically communicate that the car has a broken window. Something is missing in this example that prevents it from being an instance of irony. The missing element, according to Grice, is the expression of an attitude on the part of the speaker.

This has long been accepted in the pragmatics of irony following Grice. Every pragmatic approach to irony has attempted to account for this attitude expressed by the ironic speaker. If we examine Grice's formulation again, we can venture that he considered this attitude to always be in the negative range – as negative as are indignation, contempt and hostile or derogatory judgements. However, this is a condition rarely accepted by subsequent theories. I will return to this controversy in Chapter 5.

(ii)   To Speak Ironically Is to Pretend

> To be ironical is, among other things, to pretend (as the etymology suggests), and while one wants the pretense to be recognized as such, to announce it as a pretense would spoil the effect. (Grice 1967b/89: 54)

With this brief claim regarding the ironic speaker's pretence, Grice created a new branch of the pragmatics of irony. Many authors have subsequently attempted to account for verbal irony in terms of pretence. I will focus on them in Chapter 4. As for Grice, he acknowledged the place of pretence in irony but provided no further hints on the issue.[6]

(iii)   There Is No Such Thing as an Ironical Tone of Voice

> I am also doubtful whether the suggested vehicle of signification, the ironical tone, exists as a specific tone; I suspect that an ironical tone is always a contemptuous tone, or an amused tone, or some other tone connected with one or more particular feelings or attitudes; what qualifies such a tone as ironical is that it appears, on this and other occasions, when an ironical remark is made. (Grice 1967b/89: 54)

Grice was interested in the existence of the alleged ironic tone of voice, as have been all subsequent authors working on the pragmatics of irony. Ironic speakers' special tone is one of the features tradition-ally associated with irony, as we shall note in Section 6.2. There are

---

[6] Nevertheless, 'to pretend' and 'to make as if to say' appear to be close synonyms. See Section 4.2, where it is noted that to make as if to say can be viewed as parallel to the weak use of the notion of pretence.

2.2 Problems

different views and explanations of the issue depending on the theoretical standpoint adopted. As for Grice, he appeared inclined to deny that there may be a special tone of voice, although he was not very conclusive on the subject.

Activity 2.1B   Grice's Further Notes

Review your irony samples, and test the further elements of irony I have just detailed.

1. Did the speaker convey a certain attitude? Is it a negative type of attitude?
2. Would you say that the speaker is pretending?
3. Try to imagine the speaker uttering what she uttered. Did she use a special tone of voice?

Discussion

(0)   That was a clumsy woman driving.

1. *Yes.* Maia has definitely conveyed an attitude of reproof to Ku. It is a negative type of attitude.
2. If we consider pretence to be similar to acting someone else's part, then it appears adequate to describe Maia as pretending to be Ku criticizing a woman for driving clumsily.
3. It appears plausible to imagine the speaker making the utterance using a completely normal tone as well as an exaggerated (maybe surprised) tone.

2.2 PROBLEMS

Grice's account has the advantage of capturing the classical and pretheoretical conception of irony, but it also exhibits certain very basic weaknesses. The main criticisms his account has received arise from the 'echoic account' of irony, a theory proposed by Dan Sperber and Deirdre Wilson (on which I will focus in Chapter 3).

Certain aspects of Grice's account are controversial, including in particular the issue of the critical nature of irony. Grice's claims suggest that we should understand irony as always conveying a negative attitude, but this is a claim most theories are not prepared to accept, as they assert that the attitude expressed in irony can also be positive.

26   2 IRONY AS OPPOSITION

However, this controversy is not resolved, and whether Grice was in fact wrong in this aspect has yet to be determined (see Chapter 5).

Furthermore, a number of the alleged limitations of the Gricean account are due to the brevity of his notes on irony. While he touched on several important aspects of the phenomenon, he did not develop many of them, and we can thus discern a number of loose ends in his account. He did not explain, for instance, in what sense we should understand ironic speech as a type of pretence. Moreover, as noted earlier, he was not very conclusive with regard to the issue of the ironic speaker's tone of voice. However, most remarkably, he included the notion of the speaker making as if to say without fully explaining what it meant. I will elaborate on this issue in Section 2.2.1.

Thus there are certain elements that Grice included in his account of irony that he never fully explained. Hence, they become problematic when attempting to fit them into the machinery. This is one of Grice's weaknesses regarding irony. These issues have generated extensive debate, both in favour of and against the Gricean view. However, there is another central issue that questions the very foundations of Grice's approach and appears impossible to escape: it has been noted that his ideas fail to explain the rich variety of ironic cases that we observe in everyday communication. I will focus on this aspect in Sections 2.2.2 and 2.2.3. Then, in Section 2.2.4, I will elaborate on another issue that affects the Gricean approach; that is, ironic utterances appear pointless and uninformative if we adhere to his claims and explanations.

2.2.1 To Make as if to Say

Grice included a concept in his description of ironic communication on which he did not elaborate. He claimed that the speaker, when being ironic, *makes as if to say* the literal meaning of the utterance, likely attempting to avoid the contradiction issue he would otherwise face. While we can sense why Grice included this phrase in his explanations of irony, the lack of further elucidation weakens his account. In particular, it is difficult to envision how we can fit Grice's claims regarding irony within his general theory of implicatures because that theory appears to be grounded in the concept of *saying*.

Grice classified irony as a case of particularized implicature. Nonetheless, the Gricean theory of implicatures considers *what is said* to be the input for implicatures,[7] and because, according to Grice, in irony the speaker does not say but makes as if to say, we

---

[7] At least for the implicatures generated via the flagrant violation of the maxim of quality, because they allude to the truth of what the speaker says.

2.2 Problems 27

cannot discern how the ironic speaker can possibly be able to implicate anything.

Grice may have become aware of this issue because at a certain point he explained that it is also possible to implicate something when we make as if to say, 'A man who, by (in, when) saying (or making as if to say) that p has implicated that q' (Grice 1967a/89: 30). Thus, implicating without saying would no longer be a problem.

However, this step brings us to a new dead end: according to Grice, ironic speakers exploit the first maxim of quality, and it is by this blatant flouting that they can implicate something. However, this maxim consists of not *saying* what one believes to be false, and therefore, it is not clear how ironic speakers could be able to flout it because, again, they do not say but make as if to say. Therefore, even if we admitted that by following Grice we could arrive at certain implicatures without saying the literal meaning of the utterance, we would not be able to explain how these implicatures are generated in the case of irony because there can be no flouting of the maxim of quality when nothing has been said.

2.2.2 Irony with No Flouting

The most significant issue with the Gricean account of irony may be that it appears unable to explain certain types of ironic examples. For example, there exist cases in which the speaker is ironic, although she does not flout the first maxim of quality – in other words, cases in which the speaker says something she believes to be true. Let us consider one of these cases.

> During the precept, Danny was dominating the discussion. He certainly seemed to be familiar with the subject, but he was obnoxious in the way he showed off his knowledge. Jesse, one of Danny's classmates, said:
>
> (5) You sure know a lot.
>
> (Kumon-Namakura et al. 1995: 7)

The speaker in this example can certainly believe that Danny knows a lot and still be ironic when uttering **(5)** in this context. It appears, then, that a speaker can be ironic without flouting the first maxim of quality. This is a problem that directly threatens the Gricean view, as his idea of irony relies precisely on the speaker putting forward something she believes not to be true. It is not a problem that we can easily conceal because examples of this type are common among ironic cases:

28   2 IRONY AS OPPOSITION

Bill is a neurotically cautious driver who keeps his petrol tank full, never fails to indicate when turning and repeatedly scans the horizon for possible dangers. His companion says:

(6) I really appreciate cautious drivers.

(Wilson 2006: 1726)

A mother says to her teenage son:

(7) I love children who keep their rooms clean

just as she has discovered that her son, once again, failed to clean his room.

(Gibbs & O'Brien 1991: 525)

Another problem for Grice is that in these types of cases speakers cannot be taken to implicate the contradictory of what they make as if to say – as they do believe what they make as if to say to be true, and therefore, they cannot believe the contradictory meaning. It is evident, then, that Grice's machinery (or the classical view of irony in terms of opposition) cannot address these instances of irony.

2.2.3 Non-Declarative Irony

Furthermore, speakers can be ironic with utterances of non-declarative sentences, such as questions, advice, promises and so on.

Bill is a neurotically cautious driver who keeps his petrol tank full, never fails to indicate when turning and repeatedly scans the horizon for possible dangers. His companion says:

(8) Don't forget to use your indicator.

(9) Do you think we should stop for petrol?

(Wilson 2006: 1726)

A Gricean has two problems here. First, she must explain how these speakers can flout the maxim of quality: how is it possible to say something you believe to be false when you are not, strictly speaking, saying anything, but asking a question or giving advice? Utterances **(8)** and **(9)** could not possibly be blatantly false because no imperative or interrogative utterance can be either true or false. Second, she must explain what the opposite of these literal meanings would be. It does not appear reasonable to maintain

2.2 Problems 29

that these speakers are communicating that the hearer should forget to use the indicator or asking whether they should not stop for petrol.

However, this problem does not belong to Grice's view of irony in particular but to a general limitation of Grice's theory of implicatures.[8] An attempt to overcome this limitation and develop Grice's theory in this direction may be found in the 'speech act theory' of irony, which I will address in Section 2.3.1.

In sum, Grice's main problem is that his conception of verbal irony as a figure of speech in which the speaker always communicates the opposite of the literal meaning cannot cover the significantly varied types of irony that occur in conversation.

2.2.4 The Point of Irony

The Gricean account of irony has often been criticized because it cannot explain certain types of ironic utterances, as I explained earlier. However, Grice's approach suffers from another shortcoming that has not garnered as much attention and should be noted here. The problem is that even in the cases in which Grice's ideas appear to be applicable (ironic utterances in which the speaker does flout the maxim of quality and by which she indeed communicates the opposite), it is difficult to make sense of such cases by merely adhering to Grice's claims. Moreover, it appears that accounts after Grice inherit this shortcoming as well.

Let us consider Grice's ironic example again:

> X, with whom A has been on close terms until now, has betrayed a secret of A's to a business rival. A and his audience both know this. A says:
>
> (3) X is a fine friend.
>
> (Grice 1967a/89: 34)

Furthermore, let us recall Grice's explanation for this ironic utterance:

> It is perfectly obvious to A and his audience that what A has said or has made as if to say is something he does not believe, and the audience knows that A knows that this is obvious to the audience. So, unless A's utterance is entirely pointless, A must be trying to get across some other proposition than the one he purports to be putting forward. This

---

[8] Or, at least, of the implicatures generated via the flouting of the maxim of quality, as they allude to the truth of what the speaker says.

30   2 IRONY AS OPPOSITION

> must be some obviously related proposition; the most obviously related proposition is the contradictory of the one he purports to be putting forward. (Grice 1967a/89: 34)

What Grice states is, essentially, the following: A has uttered 'X is a fine friend'. This utterance would typically be employed to *say* that X is a fine friend, but in this case it is common knowledge to A and his audience that A does not believe that X is a fine friend. Therefore, A is *making as if to say* that X is a fine friend. Thus, if A's utterance is not 'entirely pointless', there must be another proposition that the speaker is intending to communicate. This proposition is 'the most obviously related' one: the contradictory to that X is a fine friend, namely, X is not a fine friend. With that we complete the analysis of A's utterance, and it may thus be where we find the point of his utterance.

This has been accepted as a valid explanation of these types of ironic utterances in Gricean terms. A speaker utters a sentence that puts forward something she obviously does not believe, and therefore, she implicates the contradictory. However, if we examine this reasoning more closely, we will observe that we are not making much sense of ironic utterances in this way. Ironic utterances would essentially be uninformative or pointless if this was all there was to them. In fact, if the hearer realizes that the speaker is not *saying* what she appears to be saying, it is because he recognizes that the speaker does not believe what she is putting forward to be true. Even so, all the hearer knows after understanding the irony is that the speaker believes the contradictory of what she is apparently saying. This appears to make the utterance pointless. Let us outline the hearer's reasoning to view it more clearly:

- A has uttered 'X is a fine friend'.
- A has made as if to say that p (*that X is a fine friend*) because A does not believe that p, and this is common knowledge.
- Therefore, A has implicated that $\neg p$, that is, *that X is not a fine friend*.[9]

A hearer, when understanding an ironic utterance, must know that the speaker does not believe such-and-such and merely concludes that the speaker communicates not-such-and-such. Ironic utterances would have a minimum (if any) informative effect according to this picture. This would make ironic utterances pointless, and this clashes with the general picture of ironic communication, particularly if we take into account that being ironic entails risks, as I will explain in Chapter 6.

---

[9] Garmendia & Korta 2007: 5. For further details on the point of irony, Grice's problem and a possible solution, see that article as well.

2.3 *Some Developments* 31

Activity 2.2   Grice's Problems

Let us continue examining the examples of irony you selected in Chapter 1. It is time to assess whether they pose a problem for the Gricean view; that is, whether they belong to one of the two problematic groups.

1. Does the speaker believe that what she made as if to say is true?
2. Are any of your three ironic utterances non-declarative (i.e. question, advice, acknowledgement, etc.)?

Discussion

(0)   That was a clumsy woman driving.

1. *No.* In my sample, the speaker makes as if to say something that she evidently does not believe.
2. *No.* My sample is a declarative. (In any case, we can easily imagine an alternative case in which Maia asks an ironic question, such as, 'Isn't it comforting to see one's convictions reinforced?'.)

2.3   SOME DEVELOPMENTS

Several theories have developed Grice's ideas on irony in different directions. Irony has been explained as a form of insincere speech act (Amante 1981; Haverkate 1990), an *asif*-phenomenon (Garmendia 2011, 2013) or an indirect negation (Giora 1995; Giora et al. 1998), among others.

2.3.1   Speech Act Theory

Speech act theory (Austin 1962; Searle 1969) can be used to develop Grice's theory beyond utterances of declarative sentences. Among the authors working on irony within this branch of pragmatics, David J. Amante and Henk Haverkate are particularly noteworthy.

While Grice stated that every conversation exchange followed certain principles and maxims, speech act theory maintains that each type of speech act has underlying conditions that speakers are expected to follow. These conditions include the sincerity condition the speaker is presumed to follow, which is differently formulated for each type of speech act. For instance, the sincerity condition for

32   2 IRONY AS OPPOSITION

questions is that the speaker wants the information she is soliciting; the sincerity condition for advice is that the speaker believes that her advice will benefit the hearer; the sincerity condition for requests is that the speaker wants the hearer to perform the action she requests, and so on (Searle 1969: 66–67).

Ironic utterances, whatever their speech act category, are always insincere: the speaker breaks the sincerity condition of the speech act in question. Thus the speaker who ironically asks a question does not really want to obtain the information she is soliciting; the speaker who gives advice ironically does not really believe that her advice will benefit the hearer; and so on.

From this perspective, this approach develops Grice's idea of the flouting of a maxim and generalizes it to cases beyond declaratives. The speaker's flouting of the maxim of quality could be viewed, in fact, as the particular case of declarative sentences in which the speaker breaks the sincerity condition of assertions: that the speaker believes the propositional content of her utterance.

There is another element that the speech act account adds to the characterization of irony: insincerity in a speech act can be either transparent or non-transparent. An example of the latter is a lie. A transparent instance of insincerity is what we find in an ironic speech act. This allusion to irony's transparency may parallel Grice's specification that ironic speakers' flouting of the maxim must be *blatant*.

With the breaking of the sincerity condition, on the one hand, and the transparency, on the other, the speech act theory could thus explain cases of irony such as the following, which were, as mentioned earlier, problematic for Grice:

> Bill is a neurotically cautious driver who keeps his petrol tank full, never fails to indicate when turning and repeatedly scans the horizon for possible dangers. His companion says:
>
> (8) Don't forget to use your indicator.
>
> (9) Do you think we should stop for petrol?
>
> (Wilson 2006: 1726)

Utterance **(8)** is a piece of advice, but in this ironic setting the speaker does not believe that her advice will benefit the hearer – she breaks the sincerity condition of advice, and she does so in a transparent way. Utterance **(9)** is a question, but the speaker does

2.3 Some Developments

not want the information she is soliciting; that is, she is not genuinely wondering whether they should stop for petrol – she is breaking the sincerity condition for questions, and she is doing so transparently.

The authors of speech act theory appear to have overcome one of the limitations of the Gricean approach, but the Gricean view also had several other difficulties, which proponents of the speech act theory of irony have inherited. In particular, they must still explain the ironic cases in which no condition is broken – examples such as **(5)** 'You sure know a lot', **(6)** 'I really appreciate cautious drivers' and **(7)** 'I love children who keep their rooms clean', which appear not to break the sincerity condition. Moreover, they face the challenge of explaining what the point of irony is because, in this approach as well, ironic utterances appear to be mere reminders of prior knowledge.[10]

2.3.2 The *Asif*-Theory

My proposal for explaining ironic communication is the '*asif*-theory', an account that could be considered neo-Gricean[11] but is more specifically grounded in critical pragmatics (Korta & Perry 2007a, 2007b, 2011), a pragmatic approach to reference and communication.

The *asif*-theory aims to develop from (and correct) Grice's ideas on irony and to articulate a fully fledged theory that explains ironic communication. From Grice, the *asif*-theory inherits the view of irony as essentially negative, the notion of the speaker's making as if to say and the claim that ironic content is always implicated. In addition, however, the *asif*-theory aspires to accommodate the strongest points of the echoic and pretence accounts – I will explain how it accomplishes this in Section 6.4, after discussing the details of the echoic and pretence theories.

Grice's approach to irony provided an invaluable contribution to the pragmatic field and particularly to the analysis of ironic communication – this is beyond any doubt. Nevertheless, it also had limitations because Grice did not develop certain concepts, made controversial claims and could not explain certain varieties of irony, as I noted in Section 2.2. The *asif*-theory draws from the breakthroughs that we owe to the Gricean account but also offers a solution to the three types of weaknesses it faces.

---

[10] See Garmendia and Korta (2007) to view how the speech act theory inherits this problem detected in Grice's account.

[11] This is why I included it in this chapter, although this approach does not view irony as implicating the opposite. I believe, however, that its contribution can be better understood if compared with the theories in this first group.

34 2 IRONY AS OPPOSITION

To Make as if to Say

I use the term introduced by Grice to explain irony – I state, as he did, that ironic speakers make as if to say. However, I define the act of making as if to say in terms of basic pragmatic notions, thus developing Grice's use of the term.

The *asif*-theory starts with comparing ironic and other types of utterances. Compared with literal, sincere and non-erroneous utterances (the paradigmatic types of utterances on which pragmatics tend to focus), irony has an obvious particularity: the literal meaning of the utterance does not match the belief that the speaker intends to communicate. Thus, when a speaker intends to communicate that her house is pink, she can typically utter, 'My house is pink'; the literal meaning of this utterance matches the belief she intends to communicate – that the speaker's house is pink. In contrast, if we use Grice's ironic example, the literal meaning of A's utterance is that X is a fine friend, but this does not match the belief A intends to communicate – that X is not a fine friend because he has betrayed A.

This type of discordance is always found in irony. It is not just any type of discordance, however. Occasionally, speakers utter sentences, and their utterance's literal meaning does not match the belief they intended to communicate, but they are not aware of this mismatch. For instance, sometimes speakers make errors, such as when someone utters, 'Donald Trump is really fun', when she actually intended to communicate (and, in this case, to *say*), 'Donald Duck is really fun'. The difference between this type of mismatch and irony is that speakers who make an error do not mismatch meanings intentionally. In irony, in contrast, the discordance is always intentional on the part of the speaker – A was aware that he uttered, 'X is a fine friend', although he did not intend to communicate that X is a fine friend.

Irony always involves an intentional clash. However, so do lies. When a speaker lies, she produces an utterance whose literal meaning does not match her beliefs, as when a child utters, 'I did not eat the cake', when she knows perfectly well that she did. What distinguishes irony from lies is that the speaker must intend the hearer to recognize both the mismatch and the intention to make it recognizable; that is, the mismatch must be *overt*. Returning to the fine friend example, it is because the hearer recognizes that the speaker has intended him to recognize the discordance and the intention to make it recognizable that the hearer realizes that the speaker is being ironic – otherwise, if the hearer recognized the discordance but not the overtness, he may

2.3 Some Developments   35

have thought that the speaker was intending to deceive him by making him believe that he actually believes that X is a fine friend.

When the speaker overtly mismatches the literal meaning of her utterance and the belief she is intending to communicate is when I claim that she *makes as if to say* the literal meaning of her utterance. Thus, making as if to say is an act similar to saying but is free of commitments: the speaker does not take responsibility for believing the truth of the content she makes as if to say. With this characterization of the act of making as if to say, this theory overcomes one of the weaknesses of the Gricean view and enables the explanation of irony to better fit within a general pragmatic theory of communication.

Irony Is Always Negative

Grice's second problem was the controversial claim that irony is always negative. According to the *asif*-theory, by making as if to say the literal meaning of the utterance, the speaker implicates an ironic content. This ironic content is made up of implicatures, and it contains a criticism – the expression of a negatively evaluative attitude towards someone or something. To this latter content, the speaker is indeed committed, as every speaker is to the implicatures of her utterance. Thus, in irony we always have an overt discordance, certain implicatures and a negative attitude; these are the basic and the only necessary elements of an ironic utterance according to the *asif*-theory.

Thus this view of irony adopts Grice's suggestion regarding the negative nature of irony and makes a clear case for it. I shall focus on this issue in Chapter 5.

Irony with No Flouting

Third, Grice's main problem was his inability to account for a variety of ironic cases. The primary issue for him was to explain how there could be instances of irony in which the speaker believes in the truth of what she makes as if to say – as irony for Grice is based on the speaker making as if to say something she believes not to be true.

The *asif*-theory dismisses the flouting of the quality maxim in irony and instead proposes to analyze irony in terms of a mismatch between the literal meaning of the utterance and the speaker's motivating belief – essentially the (primary) belief that the speaker intends to communicate through her utterance. The inclusion of this latter

36   2 IRONY AS OPPOSITION

notion makes it easier to account for the cases that were problematic for Grice. Now we can acknowledge cases of irony in which the speaker believes the literal meaning to be true, provided that the belief that matches the literal meaning is not the belief that the speaker intends to communicate with her ironic utterance. Therefore, in the examples in which the speaker does not flout the maxim of quality, such as the following:

> During the precept, Danny was dominating the discussion. He certainly seemed to be familiar with the subject, but he was obnoxious in the way he showed off his knowledge. Jesse, one of Danny's classmates, said:
>
> (5) You sure know a lot.
>
> (Kumon-Namakura et al. 1995: 7)

The *asif*-theory claims that the speaker can indeed hold the belief that coincides with the literal meaning she is putting forward – in this case, that Danny knows a lot. It is only that this belief is not the one the speaker intends to communicate by uttering **(5)** in that situation, and therein arises the clash between contents. Jesse, who uttered **(5)** 'You sure know a lot', believes that Danny knows a lot, but that is not what he wants to communicate, which is that Danny is behaving arrogantly, that he should learn to remain quiet sometimes or something to that effect. With this move, the *asif*-theory is able to overcome Grice's primary obstacle to accounting for irony.

Non-Declarative Irony

While the *asif*-theory initially focuses on explaining the ironic utterances of declarative sentences, this account can also benefit from the speech act theory's development in that direction – its grounds can be generalized and applied to different types of ironic speech acts (Garmendia 2011). In this case, the speaker does not overtly reveal an intentional discordance between her motivating belief and the literal meaning of the utterance; instead, it is a certain preparatory or sincerity rule of the corresponding speech act that is intentionally and overtly violated. Thus, in **(8)**, Bill's companion overtly shows that he does not in fact doubt that Bill will use the indicator without being reminded, and in **(9)**, he makes it overtly recognizable that he does not actually want to obtain the answer to his question. In these cases, the speaker makes as if to suggest or as if to ask. In so doing, he intends to implicate something else or something different.

2.3 Some Developments

The Point of Irony

Finally, when addressing Grice's shortcomings, I have explained that the Gricean account has trouble making sense of ironic utterances because they look uninformative and pointless if we adhere to Grice's analysis. A hearer must know that the speaker does not believe p to understand that she is being ironic, but then the only thing that the hearer will obtain from the utterance is that the speaker believes that not-p.

The *asif*-theory has a direct and simple answer to this issue. In the cases that follow the Gricean pattern – utterances through which the speaker makes as if to say something that she believes to be false and communicates the opposite – the speaker typically communicates the contradictory meaning to which Grice refers, but not only. The speaker, when being ironic, typically communicates a group of implicatures, some of which are easily graspable and others more subtle.[12] This occurs in every ironic utterance, not only in those that follow Grice's pattern.

Thus A, when uttering **(3)** 'X is a fine friend', is implicating that X is not a fine friend, but not merely. He may also intend to implicate that he (A) has been a fool to believe in X, that he should not have trusted him or something to that effect. That X is not a fine friend is just one among a group of implicatures. It is obviously closely related to the literal meaning of the utterance, and thus it may have been more strongly implicated. I call it the 'bridge content' of the ironic utterance because it is the link that helps us infer other implicatures in the ironic content.

Acknowledging that the speaker, when being ironic, does not implicate only one implicature but a group of implicatures may appear to be a small and not very significant step. It is a crucial point, however, and not only for the issue of Grice's pointless irony – this idea will be useful when we address certain other elements of irony in the following chapters.

Applying all these ideas to cases of irony will help us make better sense of the phenomenon. Let us revisit the classical Gricean example:

> X, with whom A has been on close terms until now, has betrayed a secret of A's to a business rival. A and his audience both know this. A says:
>
> (3) X is a fine friend.
>
> (Grice 1967a/89: 34)

---

[12] Or, in terms of relevance theory, *weaker* and *stronger* implicatures (Carston 2002: 380).

38   2 IRONY AS OPPOSITION

A uttered, 'X is a fine friend', and the literal meaning of this utterance is that X is a fine friend. However, the hearer realizes that A does not believe that X is a fine friend – as we are told that the audience is familiar with X's betrayal – and thus recognizes that the literal meaning does not match A's beliefs. Furthermore, the hearer notices that A has made no effort to hide the mismatch and understands that the speaker has intended him to recognize both the mismatch and the intention to make it recognizable. The hearer, then, realizes that the speaker cannot be intending to communicate the literal meaning of the utterance, but something different. The literal meaning can help the hearer grasp something that the speaker intended to communicate that X is not a fine friend. This has not been explicitly communicated by the speaker; it is an implicature of his utterance **(3)**. This implicature is closely related to the literal meaning, which I called the 'bridge content' of the utterance. Following the thread of this first implicature, the hearer can grasp further implicatures: that A will no longer trust X, that A realizes that he has been a fool to trust A and so on. All these implicatures constitute the ironic content of **(3)**, and they contain a negative attitude: a criticism towards X.

2.3.3   Irony as Indirect Negation

Grice's is a two-stage model of irony: it states that there are two different meanings in every ironic utterance, one that is made as if to say and another that has been implicated. This aspect is similar to the classical conception of irony, according to which we also have two meanings in irony: what the speaker says and what she means.

Nevertheless, the view of irony as a two-stage phenomenon has been extensively debated in the pragmatics of irony. We shall note in what follows that one-stage models have been defended to account for ironic communication (the echoic account, in Chapter 3; and the pretence theory, in Chapter 4). However, first, I will focus on a somewhat intermediate proposal, which states that there are two meanings in irony but that they are not the ones Grice suggested, nor do they work in irony the way he thought.

Rachel Giora's account of irony is based on two main claims, each of which questions an assumption made by the standard two-stage views of irony. In two-stage models of irony, it is assumed that the literal meaning of the utterance is discarded once the ironic content of the utterance is grasped. In contrast, according to Giora (1995), in irony we process both the literal and the implicated meanings so that we can compute the difference between them. These two meanings are set in

2.4 Summary

a relationship of indirect negation, that is, a non-explicit form of negation, which does not use an overt negation marker. An advantage of this view is that it can accommodate different cases of irony because, while direct negation implies the opposite of what one negates in indirect negation, the product of the implicature allows for a more mitigated interpretation.

Thus in irony we have two meanings that are related in terms of indirect negation and that the hearer retains when processing the utterance. With this, Giora already departs significantly from the standard two-stage view of irony.

Furthermore, Giora's account of irony makes use of the *graded salience hypothesis*, defended by the same author with regard to a more general pragmatic application. In this line, Giora rejects the priority of literal meaning in utterance interpretation (Giora et al. 1998). Instead, she postulates that the most salient meaning is the one first captured by a hearer, whichever it is. The saliency of a meaning is determined by its conventionality, familiarity and frequency. Thus it can be the case that the most salient meaning of a certain utterance is not its literal meaning, in which case the most salient meaning will have priority of interpretation and not the literal one, as has been assumed traditionally.

Salient meanings are activated before less salient meanings are grasped, which, applied to irony, implies that the non-ironic meaning will generally (but not always) be the first one activated (because it is the more conventional, familiar and frequent meaning), and only then will the ironic meaning be derived. Moreover, the hearer will retain the non-ironic meaning of the utterance so that she can compute how it differs from the ironic meaning it indirectly negates.

A consequence of this view is that irony may take longer to process than non-figurative meanings, a possibility that has been long debated by experimental approaches to ironic communication.

2.4 SUMMARY

Grice's contribution to the pragmatics of irony has been undeniable in that he signalled the main issues to be explained and clarified by subsequent theories. Thus most pragmatic accounts of irony have followed the threads suggested by the Gricean approach.

The Gricean view formalizes the classical idea of irony we typically share and compiles many features traditionally associated with ironic communication: the importance of the ironic speaker expressing

40 2 IRONY AS OPPOSITION

a certain attitude, the existence of a special ironic tone of voice, the etymological relationship between irony and pretence and, in particular, the central idea of irony as opposition between meanings.

Grice was brief in his statements on irony, and a general Gricean theory of irony would require developments and corrections. Several authors have worked on this endeavour, elaborating on Grice's claims in different directions. In this chapter, I have touched on three different theoretical proposals that amend the original account in several aspects but can certainly still be considered Gricean in essence.

In what follows, I focus on two approaches that offer distinct views of irony: first, the echoic account by Sperber and Wilson and, second, the pretence theories of irony.

2.5 SUGGESTED READING

2.5.1 Grice

Grice's notes on irony can be found in these two lectures compiled in his 1989 book:

Grice, H. P. 1967a/89. Logic and conversation. In *The Logic of Grammar*, ed. D. Davidson & G. Harman, 1975, 64–75. Encino: Dickenson. Also in *Syntax and Semantics 3: Speech Acts*, ed. P. Cole & J. L. Morgan, 1975, 41–58. New York: Academic Press. Reprinted in Grice (1989), 22–40.
Grice, H. P. 1967b/89. Further notes on logic and conversation. In *Syntax and Semantics 9: Pragmatics*, ed. P. Cole, 1978, 113–27. New York: Academic Press. Reprinted in Grice (1989), 41–57.
Grice, H. P. 1989. *Studies in the Way of Words*. Cambridge, MA: Harvard University Press.

2.5.2 Grice's Problems

The echoic account has dedicated many pages to identifying the weaknesses of Grice's view of irony. Most of them can be found in the chapter devoted to irony in Wilson and Sperber's (2012) book. An analysis of these criticisms and a possible answer are offered in my 2015 article.

Garmendia, J. 2015. A (neo-)Gricean account of irony: an answer to relevance theory. *International Review of Pragmatics* 7: 40–79.
Wilson, D. & D. Sperber. 2012. *Meaning and Relevance*. Cambridge: Cambridge University Press.

2.5 Suggested Reading

2.5.3 Some Developments

In addition to the three (neo-)Gricean accounts I have mentioned here, several other theories propose to analyze irony in terms of certain notions more distantly related to the idea of opposition, such as contrast, inversion or inappropriateness. Attardo's article, in addition to introducing his own account, offers a clear general perspective on the existing pragmatic theories of irony.

Attardo, S. 2000. Irony as relevant inappropriateness. *Journal of Pragmatics* 32: 793–826.

Colston, H. L. & J. O'Brien. 2000. Contrast and pragmatics in figurative language: anything understatement can do, irony can do better. *Journal of Pragmatics* 32: 1557–83.

Rodríguez-Rosique, S. 2013. The power of inversion: irony, from utterance to discourse. In *Irony and Humour: From Pragmatics to Discourse*, ed. L. Ruiz-Gurillo & M. B. Alvarado-Ortega, 17–38. Amsterdam: John Benjamins.

3 Irony as Echo

Irony is a recurrent subject in 'relevance theory', a theory of communication proposed by Dan Sperber and Deirdre Wilson (1986/95). This theory defends the view of verbal irony as an echo, distancing itself from the standard and more traditional approach to irony as opposition. Since Sperber and Wilson first presented their 'echoic account' in 1981, they have devoted several studies to the analysis of irony (Sperber 1984; Sperber & Wilson 1998; Wilson 2006, 2009, 2013; Wilson & Sperber 1992, 2012). The echoic account has developed over time, and these authors have substantially elaborated on the fundamental notions of the theory.

This account has touched on every aspect of ironic communication. The work of these authors on irony mostly focuses on three general goals. First, they intend to show that the classical account (and, in particular, its Gricean reconstruction) does not properly explain ironic communication. Second, they claim that the echoic account is a sufficient alternative for explaining ironic utterances. Finally, they attempt to show that the echoic and pretence accounts are distinguishable both theoretically and empirically. They insist that echoic use is essential in standard irony, whereas pretence is not.

In Chapter 2, I explained the main weaknesses Sperber and Wilson discern in the Gricean approach, and presently I will explain their own account in depth. In Chapter 4, I will focus on the 'pretence theory' of irony and will describe how it compares with the echoic view.

3.1 THE ECHOIC ACCOUNT

Sperber and Wilson are the authors of the echoic view of irony. Their main contribution has been to bring the notion of echo to the fore, as the standard view of irony as a case of opposition had few competing

3.1 The Echoic Account

alternatives. They claim that irony is essentially echoic, although the exact formulation of their definition of irony as echo has changed over the years. I will approach their proposal as they present it in their latest works.

> ### A Short History of Echo
>
> - In Sperber & Wilson (1981), the authors describe irony as a case of echoic mention, in which the speaker evokes an attitude (of rejection) toward the proposition mentioned.
> - In Sperber (1984), irony continues to be defined as an *implicit* echoic mention of meaning conveying a derogatory attitude towards the meaning mentioned. The author analyzes the alternative proposal of the pretence theory but defends the superiority of the echoic account.
> - In Sperber and Wilson (1986/95), the authors replace the notion of mention with a notion of interpretive resemblance, and thereafter (including Wilson & Sperber (1992)), echoic utterances are analyzed as echoic 'interpretations' of an attributed thought or utterance and verbal irony as a variety of echoic interpretation.
> - In Sperber and Wilson (1998), the authors uphold that irony must always be echoic (in response to Hamamoto (1998), Seto (1998) and Yamanashi (1998)).
> - In Wilson (2006, 2009, 2013) and Wilson and Sperber (2012), irony is presented as a case of echoic 'attribution'.

In terms of relevance theory, utterances are used to represent a speaker's thoughts, which they resemble in content. Any utterance, the authors claim, can be used to represent things in two different ways:

- **Descriptively:** when they represent a certain state of affairs in virtue of its propositional form being true of that state of affairs.
- **Interpretively:** when they represent another representation, which also has a propositional form – a thought, for instance – in virtue of a resemblance between the two propositional forms (Sperber & Wilson 1986/95: 228–29).

A note should be made here of the use of the notion of resemblance when defining interpretive uses of language. The propositional form of the utterance used interpretively must merely resemble *closely enough* the propositional form of the representation of which it is

44   3 IRONY AS ECHO

intended to be an interpretation. Identity, they say, is just a limiting case of resemblance.

The following short dialogues illustrate this distinction between descriptions and interpretations. Utterance **(10)** represents the state of affairs of being a lovely day for a picnic, whereas utterance **(11)** represents Peter's previous utterance.

> MARY: What shall we do today?
> PETER: (10) It is a lovely day for a picnic.
> JANE: Do you have plans for today?
> MARY: (11) It is a lovely day for a picnic, Peter thinks.

When the utterance represents a thought that is about another thought (that it resembles in content), which the speaker attributes to a source other than herself at the current time, Wilson and Sperber call it an 'attributive' use of language. Attributive uses are thus a subcategory of interpretive uses. Mary, as she was representing a thought that she attributes to Peter, made an attributive interpretation of it.

Reporting utterances or thoughts may be the most easily identifiable attributive use of language. The goal of this indirect form of speech is mainly to inform the hearer regarding the content of the utterance/thought that the speaker is attributing to someone else. Mary's intention when uttering **(11)** was to inform Jane regarding the content of Peter's previous utterance – Mary reported Peter's utterance.

However, language can also be used attributively with the primary intention of conveying the speaker's attitude towards the attributed thought/utterance. These are the cases in which Sperber and Wilson say that the speaker makes an echoic use of language. Echoes are, therefore, a subclass of the attributive use of language.

When producing an echoic utterance, the speaker can convey an array of attitudes: she can show acceptance of the attributed thought **(12)**, she can demonstrate that she has reservations regarding its veracity **(13)** or she can openly reject it **(14)**, as Mary demonstrates when replying to Peter:

> MARY: What shall we do today?
> PETER: (10) It is a lovely day for a picnic.
> MARY: (12) It is a lovely day for a picnic! Yay! It has been too long since we have been to the valley!
>
> (13) It is a lovely day for a picnic. Have you checked the weather forecast?

3.1 The Echoic Account

(14) It is a lovely day for a picnic. It is *always* a lovely day for a picnic for you.

What distinguishes irony from other echoes is that when being ironic, the speaker always conveys a 'dissociative attitude'; that is, the speaker rejects the attributed thought as ludicrously false (or blatantly inadequate in other ways). With this, these authors attempt to capture the importance of the attitude conveyed by ironic speakers, which, as mentioned earlier, has been a central issue in the pragmatics of irony. Sperber and Wilson claim that this attitude is always of the dissociative type, but they acknowledge diversity in this type of attitude:

> Dissociative attitudes themselves vary quite widely, falling anywhere on a spectrum from amused tolerance through various shades of resignation or disappointment to contempt, disgust, outrage or scorn. The attitudes prototypical of verbal irony are generally seen as coming from the milder, or more controlled, part of the range. However, there is not cut-off point between dissociative attitudes that are prototypically ironical and those that are not. (Wilson & Sperber, 2012: 130)

A paradigmatic case of an ironic echo, in which the speaker conveys her dissociative attitude towards an utterance that she attributes to

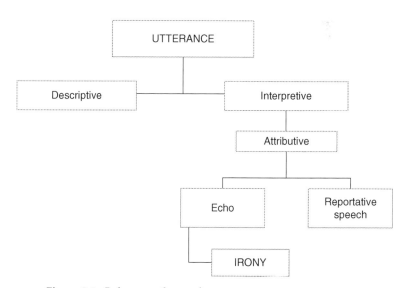

Figure 3.1 Relevance theory: language uses

46   3 IRONY AS ECHO

someone other than herself (at the current time), is shown in Sperber and Wilson's traditional example of irony:

PETER: It's a lovely day for a picnic.

They go for a picnic and it rains.

MARY (sarcastically):

(15) It's a lovely day for a picnic, indeed.

(Sperber & Wilson 1986/95: 239)

Echoes are naturally identified when they are directed towards an immediately preceding utterance – as in **(12)**, **(13)** and **(14)** – but a speaker can also echo a more distant utterance – as in **(15)** – or even tacitly attributed but unexpressed thoughts. Moreover, attributive utterances can be used to inform the audience regarding the content of thoughts or utterances attributed to 'certain types of people, or people in general. These may have their roots in culturally defined social, moral or aesthetic norms, or general human hopes or aspirations' (Wilson & Sperber 2012: 130). The speaker can make use of these diverse degrees of echoing when she intends to be ironic as well, for example:

SUE (pointing to Jack, who has become a total nuisance after drinking some wine):

(16) As they say, a glass of wine is good for you!

(Wilson & Sperber 2012: 130)

In this case, Sue is not echoing a thought or utterance that someone has entertained in particular or said immediately before but a culturally defined belief that she shares with her audience. She is echoing that belief while she dissociates herself from it.

In sum, according to the echoic account, ironic utterances represent a thought of the speaker that is about a thought/utterance (more or less distant and expressed or unexpressed) that the speaker attributes to a source (particular or more general) other than herself at the current time. The speaker's intention is to convey her dissociative attitude towards the thought that she is echoing.

According to this view, we do not have a pair of meanings in irony, as the Gricean view claims, namely, one that is made as if to say and another that is implicated. In irony, then, there is only one meaning,

3.1 The Echoic Account 47

Activity 3.1A The Echoic Account

I have explained the basic ideas of the echoic account of irony, so let us apply them to our examples. Review your irony samples and try to answer the following questions. As before, you can view the answers for my sample below.

1. Is your utterance an echo of an utterance/thought that the speaker attributes to someone other than herself at the current time?
2. Does the speaker dissociate herself from that which she is echoing?
3. Does the utterance echo an utterance/thought that is attributable to a specific person? (It may also be the case that it is attributable to a general source, such as human expectations or social norms.)
4. Is this source close to the utterance (immediately preceding in the context) or more distant?

Discussion

(0) That was a clumsy woman driving.

1. *Yes.* Maia is echoing an utterance that she attributes to Ku.
2. *Yes.* Maia is dissociating herself from that which she is echoing.
3. *Yes.* The utterance echoes an utterance easily attributable to Ku.
4. It is not an immediately preceding utterance or, at least, it does not have to be. It is enough to know that Ku typically claims that women drive terribly in order to understand Maia's irony.

---

towards which the speaker expresses her dissociative attitude. The echoic account is a one-stage theory of irony, in contrast to Grice's (and the traditional) two-stage view.

Relevance theory thus explains the basics of ironic communication in terms of echo. In addition, Sperber and Wilson touched on the three aspects of irony Grice signalled as being crucial in the pragmatic analysis of this phenomenon: the alleged negative nature of irony, the relationship between irony and pretence and the ironic speaker's tone of voice. These authors' views diverge from Grice's with regard to all three of them.

(i) Irony Can Also Be Positive

When analyzing Grice's approach to irony, I have noted that he suggests that irony is (always) negative; that is, when being ironic, we

48   3 IRONY AS ECHO

always convey a negative attitude. Sperber and Wilson do not agree. They contend that there are cases of irony that do not convey something negative – instances of positive irony. However, according to Wilson and Sperber, there is a normative bias in ironic communication: irony is typically used to criticize, and only in special circumstances is it used to praise. They present the following pair of examples to illustrate what is called irony's 'asymmetry issue':

Nancy and her friend Jane were planning a trip to the beach.

'It's probably going to rain tomorrow', said Jane, who worked for a local TV station as a meteorologist.

The next day was a warm and sunny one.
As she looked out of the window, Nancy said:

(17) This certainly is awful weather.

(Wilson & Sperber 2012: 127)

Nancy and her friend Jane were planning a trip to the beach.

'The weather should be nice tomorrow', said Jane, who worked for a local TV station as a meteorologist.

The next day was a cold and stormy one.
As she looked out of the window, Nancy said:

(18) This certainly is beautiful weather.

(Wilson & Sperber 2012: 128)

The second scene exemplifies a traditional instance of negative irony: Nancy appears to be saying that it is beautiful weather, but she is actually communicating through irony that it is cold and stormy, awful weather for a trip to the beach. This example works as the traditional ironic cases we have considered thus far: irony used to blame and irony showing an apparently positive value while intending to convey something negative.

In contrast, the first scene would be an example of positive irony: Nancy appears to be complaining or regretting that the weather is awful, while she is ironically communicating that the weather is warm and sunny and ideal for a trip to the beach. This is an instance of what has typically been called 'positive irony': irony used to praise (in this case, to praise the good weather) and showing an apparently negative value while intending to convey something positive.

3.1 The Echoic Account

Sperber and Wilson accept both cases as instances of irony. Thus, they assume that positive irony exists – something that Grice may not accept, as I have explained. However, they also acknowledge that irony is *typically* used to criticize and that cases of praising irony are scarce. The challenge for a pragmatic theory thus consists in explaining why the latter type of example is far more common than examples of the former; that is, the challenge is to explain why irony is typically negative and why positive irony is scarce or why irony is frequently used to criticize and only in special circumstances used to praise.

Wilson and Sperber's explanation is as follows. They claim that in the first example, as it is a positive irony, utterance **(17)** counts as ironical only (or, at least, more probably) if Jane's utterance is present; that is, only if Jane had predicted that it would rain would Nancy sound ironic when uttering **(17)** 'This certainly is awful weather' when the sun is shining.

In contrast, in the second example, which is negative irony, Nancy's utterance **(18)** 'This certainly is beautiful weather' would be equally ironical with or without Jane's utterance, namely, regardless of whether Jane wrongly predicted the weather. Additionally, this may be explained by the fact that positive irony in which the ironic utterance has an apparent negative value is appropriate only when doubt has been previously entertained or expressed, whereas negative irony does not require prior doubt. Thus, positive irony requires 'special circumstances', which is why it is scarcer than negative irony.

Wilson and Sperber (2012: 127) offer another example to illustrate the asymmetry issue of irony. When someone is moving clumsily, it is easy to ironically say, 'How graceful!' – we do not require anything special in the context to make the irony work. In contrast, when someone is moving gracefully, an ironic utterance such as 'How clumsy!' would not work so easily. According to Wilson and Sperber, it would require special circumstances to make that utterance work as a positive irony – for example, if someone had predicted that this person would perform clumsily. Thus, this case shows again that positive irony has stronger requirements than negative irony, which would explain why the former is scarcer than the latter.

Thus, unlike Grice, Sperber and Wilson assume that there do exist cases of positive irony. They also accept that this type of case is scarcer

50   3 IRONY AS ECHO

than negative irony, but they are able to explain in terms of echo why this asymmetry exists. There are other authors who provide different explanations for the same issue. I shall return to this point in Chapter 5.

(ii) To Speak Ironically Is Not to Pretend

Grice mentioned the importance of the notion of pretence when accounting for irony. He did not develop this claim, but others have subsequently. Sperber and Wilson, in contrast, have devoted several works to defending that what we find in irony is echo and not pretence. I will focus on the debate between echoists and pretenders after I introduce the basics of the pretence theory in Chapter 4.

(iii) Ironic Speakers' Tone of Voice

Sperber and Wilson acknowledge that the ironic speaker has a characteristic tone of voice. This tone of voice, they claim, is a clue that the speaker uses to signal her dissociative attitude towards the utterance or thought that she is echoing. The ironic speaker thus does not abandon her own voice and replace it with the voice of the person whose utterance/thought she is echoing, as claimed by advocates of the pretence theory, as we shall see in Chapter 4. In the cases in which the speaker does imitate the voice of who she is echoing, a parodic tone of voice (that of mimicking) accompanies the proper ironic tone, according to Sperber and Wilson.

According to the Echoic Account, then, the ironic speaker makes use of a special tone of voice in order to signal her relationship to the thought/utterance she echoes. This tone of voice is always of the negative type (even in the cases of positive irony), because it stands for the mocking, sceptical or contemptuous attitude that the speaker is expressing towards the echoed thought/utterance (Wilson & Sperber 2012: 143–144).

Sperber and Wilson appear to disagree with Grice on this point as well. However, appearances can be deceiving. What Grice claimed was that there is no such thing as an ironic tone of voice, merely a certain tone connected with a particular feeling or attitude that appears on certain occasions when something is conveyed ironically. What Sperber and Wilson claim, instead, is that there is typically a tone of voice that stands for a certain attitude and that this may be what is considered to be the ironic speaker's tone of voice. Thus, they apparently only disagree on a superfluous or terminological level.

3.1 *The Echoic Account* 51

Activity 3.1B More on Echo

You have already analyzed the speaker's attitude, pretence and tone of voice in Activity 2.1B. If you noted in any of your samples that the speaker expresses an attitude that is not negative, review that example and ask yourself the following questions:

1. Does the utterance echo a wrong prediction or a similar 'special' circumstance?
2. If you answered affirmatively, is that previous circumstance a requirement for the irony in your case? That is, would your example work if we removed the previous circumstance (the wrong prediction or similar circumstance)?

Discussion

In my sample, Maia's reproof of Ku is evident. However, we can modify the example to have an instance of positive irony: let us say that Ku (who always claims that women are terrible drivers) witnesses a woman elegantly maneuvring a car into a small and awkward parking spot. Ku himself then exclaims,

(0')   That was a clumsy woman driving.

In this case, Ku would be echoing an utterance that he attributes to himself at another time and dissociating himself from it. He would also be praising the female driver via his ironic criticism. Let me answer the preceding questions considering this variant of the example.

1. *Yes.* It echoes the speaker's claim that women drive terribly.
2. *Yes.* The utterance would not work as smoothly if Ku had not predicted that women drive terribly. (In that case, we could understand Ku's positive ironic remark as echoing the social prejudice that women drive more poorly than men – at least in the societies in which this sexist assumption exists. However, again, that positive irony would not work if the shared and general prediction did not exist.)

Experimental Support

Sperber and Wilson claim that experimental data support their echoic theory of irony (Wilson 2009, 2013). They mostly rely on results obtained in experiments conducted by Francesca Happé (1993).

Hypothesis. A particularity of the echoic account is that it expects irony to involve second-order meta-representation. As in irony, we always have a thought that is about another thought. As a result, only hearers with the capacity to understand second-order representations (that is, to understand thoughts about thoughts) would be able to understand irony. The same would not hold for metaphor, as metaphor is not echoic.

Experiments. Happé (1993) put this hypothesis to the test. In different experiments, she tested whether the ability to perform tasks of different orders of theory of mind was correlated with the comprehension of metaphor and irony. She concluded that subjects who were able to complete first-order theory-of-mind tasks, but not second-order ones, could understand metaphor but not irony. Moreover, she detected that subjects who were able to complete both first- and second-order theory-of-mind tasks were able to understand both metaphor and irony.

Sperber and Wilson have used these results to support the echoic view of irony. If we require second-order theory-of-mind ability to understand irony but not metaphor, this would mean that irony involves thoughts about thoughts or second-order meta-representations, whereas metaphor does not, as their theory anticipates. These results would contradict Grice's predictions, as he contended that both metaphor and irony are cases of figurative meaning in which the speaker makes as if to say a literal meaning and implicates a figurative meaning. No difference thus should be expected in understanding metaphor and irony.

Further Reading

Several authors support the conclusions in favour of an echoic account of irony:

Colston, H. L. & R. W. Gibbs. 2002. Are irony and metaphor understood differently? *Metaphor and Symbol*, 17(1): 57–80.

Langdon, R., M. Coltheart, P. B. Ward & S. V. Catts. 2002. Disturbed communication in schizophrenia: the role of poor pragmatics and poor mind-reading. *Psychological Medicine* 32: 1273–84.

However, there are also those who do not perceive in these results evidence supporting the echoic view and refuting a Gricean (or pretence) account of irony:

3.2 Problems

Currie, G. 2006. Why irony is pretense. In *The Architecture of the Imagination*, ed. S. Nichols, 111–33. Oxford: Oxford University Press.

Reimer, M. 2013. Grice on irony and metaphor: discredited by the experimental evidence? *International Review of Pragmatics* 5: 1–33.

Experimental analysis of irony comprehension has proved to be a delicate issue. If you wish to explore this aspect of irony more deeply, the following readings constitute an interesting starting point:

Chevallier, C., I. Noveck, F. Happé & D. Wilson. 2011. What's in a voice? Prosody as a test case for the theory of mind account of autism. *Neuropsychologia* 49: 507–17.

Dufour, N., E. Redcay, L. Young, et al. 2013. Similar brain activation during false belief tasks in a large sample of adults with and without Autism. *PLoS ONE* 8(9): e75468.

Spotorno, N., A. Cheylus, J-B. Van Der Henst & I. A. Noveck. 2013. What's behind a P600? Integration operations during irony processing. *PLoS ONE* 8(6): e66839.

Spotorno, N., E. Koun, J. Prado, J-B. Van Der Henst & I. A. Noveck. 2012. Neural evidence that utterance-processing entails mentalizing: the case of irony. *NeuroImage* 63: 25–39.

Wang, A. T., S. S. Lee, M. Sigman & M. Dapretto. 2006. Neural basis of irony comprehension in children with autism: the role of prosody and context. *Brain* 129(4): 932–43.

3.2 PROBLEMS

The echoic account was presented as an alternative to the Gricean explanation of irony and thus overcomes several of its weaknesses. This account does not have, for example, any problem explaining ironic cases in which the speaker does not intend to communicate the opposite of the literal meaning. Neither does it have any limitation with regard to analyzing cases beyond assertives, as an echo can be produced via any utterance, whether declarative or of another form.

Similarly, Sperber and Wilson (and many of the followers of relevance theory) have devoted many pages to the analysis of irony and have developed their account in substantial detail. Thus, their conception of irony fits naturally within their general account of communication, with irony representing a particular instance of a class perfectly delimited within this theory. This makes their account of irony appear robust and consistent.

Nevertheless, considering irony to be essentially echoic presents new problems. In this section, I explain the primary weaknesses that

54   3 IRONY AS ECHO

have been associated with the echoic account. I focus first on the notion of echo and then on the idea of dissociation. There is also the issue of the dispute between the pretence and echoic accounts, but I address that in Section 4.2, after I have introduced the basics of the pretence theory of irony.

3.2.1 Echo

The first and main issue that we face when we explain irony in terms of echo is the notion of echo itself. Sperber and Wilson categorically claim that irony is always echoic and that only when the hearer can attribute the source of the echo to someone (or to people in general) will the irony work.

In certain cases, the thought or utterance that the speaker echoes is within sight, and the idea of the echo fits effortlessly. The examples of irony typically presented by the echoic account are of this type, such as the picnic example I introduced earlier.

PETER: It's a lovely day for a picnic.

They go for a picnic and it rains.

MARY (sarcastically):

(15) It's a lovely day for a picnic, indeed.

(Sperber & Wilson 1986/95: 239)

When the context makes the utterance explicit, which is subsequently echoed ironically, it appears natural to explain that case in terms of echo.

In many cases in which we do not have access to the echoed utterance in the explicit context, it is not difficult to imagine that such an utterance or thought may have existed.

MARY (after a boring party):

(19) That was fun.

(Wilson & Sperber 2012: 123)

Here Mary may be echoing an utterance that someone (even herself) may have uttered before the party or a thought that someone may have entertained regarding the party. We only have to suppose that someone (even Mary herself) had said, when mentioning the party later in the afternoon, 'The party is going to be fun' or 'We will surely enjoy the party' or something to that effect. If this is the case, Mary's ironic utterance will

3.2 Problems

remind us of this previous utterance, and we will understand that Mary is intending to communicate that suggesting that the party would be fun was a silly mistake. Mary's intention is now to echo that previous utterance/thought and express her dissociative attitude towards it.

> X, with whom A has been on close terms until now, has betrayed a secret of A's to a business rival. A and his audience both know this. A says:
>
> (3) X is a fine friend.
>
> (Grice 1967a/89: 34)

Similarly, it is not difficult to guess that before his friend betrayed him, A had at some point in times uttered that X is a fine friend or at least that he believed so until the betrayal occurred. Thus, as he is being ironic, A would now intend to echo that utterance/thought and dissociate himself from it.

At this point, echoing may simply appear to mean *repeating* (even if not in terms of identity but of resemblance) an utterance/thought already existing in the speaker's and hearer's (close) context. However, were the echo intended to be understood as such, many examples of ironic utterances would not fit easily into this theory. For instance, utterance **(19)** appears to be ironic even if no one had previously uttered or thought that the party was going to be fun – even if everybody anticipated that the party was actually going to be boring.

Sperber and Wilson are well aware of this, and they explain that when being ironic, we can also echo general human aspirations or hopes. Thus, returning to the example of the boring party, let us suppose that we had not said a word regarding the party before we attended and that the speaker had not had any expectations in its regard – she may even have been afraid that it was going to be boring. We can further imagine that the speaker and the hearer do not know each other: they happen to be waiting for the elevator after having left the dreary party. If Mary uttered **(19)** 'That was fun' in this scenario, the source of her echoic utterance would not be as obvious as it was in the original setting.

Wilson and Sperber claim at this point that Mary should be understood to be 'dissociating herself from an application (to this particular party) of a widely shared normative representation of how parties are *supposed* to go' (Wilson & Sperber 2012: 132). Thus, it appears that the echoic approach may also account for examples in which there is no clear repetition of a particular previous utterance/thought.

In any case, it has been argued that the strategy of accepting such generally shared ideas as possible sources of an echo also has certain

56 3 IRONY AS ECHO

limitations. I have elsewhere (Garmendia 2015: 66) proposed the following case:

> Mary and someone she does not know are waiting for an elevator after having left a funeral. It has been long and boring – as funerals are expected to be in their shared culture. Mary says:
>
> (20) That was fun!

Here Mary has ironically dissociated herself from the thought that the funeral was fun. However, in this example, we do not have any explicit source for this echo, and there is no shared normative representation that suggests that funerals should be fun – no expectation has failed. This type of case, I believe, would constitute a genuine problem for the advocates of the echoic account.

Similarly, Giora (1998) maintains that relevance theory cannot explain every ironic utterance in terms of echo. She provides the following example:

> We walk in a rather posh neighbourhood and come upon gorgeous Ferraris and Jaguars. I say:
>
> (21) What a junkyard!
>
> (Giora 1998: 2)

According to Giora, there is no echo in this ironic utterance because when we lack contextual information to identify an explicit antecedent, a negative statement cannot represent any type of wisdom nor anyone's particular thought.

However, the strategy of the echoic account appears to be to maintain that even in these cases we can find something that the speaker can be assumed to echo. In the case of the funeral, for instance, the speaker could be echoing the shared assumption that people prefer to spend their time doing fun things.[1] Thus, the echoic account insists that even in the cases in which the echo appears to be faint, we will find a trace of it.

Whether irony is necessarily echoic appears at this point to be an endless controversy. Sperber and Wilson appear prepared to continue defending the necessity of the echo, even if they must accept wider and lighter instances of echoes each time they face new counterexamples. They may have been aware of this possible reticence towards their echoic proposal from the beginning. In fact, they have attempted to offer a flexible, broad and accommodative definition of echo on several occasions.

---

[1] As Wilson herself explained in a personal conversation.

3.2 Problems 57

> In other words, in order to be successfully ironic, the meaning mentioned must recognizably echo a thought that has been, is being, or might be entertained or expressed by someone. Here *echo* is used in a technical sense that is wider than its ordinary sense (but not really wider than its conventional metaphorical sense). (Sperber 1984: 131)

The echo, defined thus, could include anything. One may even question whether there is any meaning that no one has ever expressed or entertained. Certainly, there is no meaning that no one *may* not ever express or entertain. The subsequent modifications of the definition of echo may have been an attempt to avoid this imprecision in the first attempts. However, this continues to be the most problematic and controversial aspect of Sperber and Wilson's theory.

3.2.2 Dissociation

I have mentioned that the echoic account overcomes a number of Grice's limitations when explaining irony. Nevertheless, there is one issue that affects the Gricean and the echoic approaches equally.

Grice holds that the ironic speaker does not believe the literal meaning of the utterance to be true – thus, she flouts the first maxim of quality when making as if to say that meaning. Hence, Grice had a problem explaining cases of irony in which the speaker believes the literal meaning of the utterance to be true.

> During the precept, Danny was dominating the discussion. He certainly seemed to be familiar with the subject, but he was obnoxious in the way he showed off his knowledge. Jesse, one of Danny's classmates, said:
>
> (5) You sure know a lot.
>
> > (Kumon-Namakura et al. 1995: 7)

> Bill is a neurotically cautious driver who keeps his petrol tank full, never fails to indicate when turning and repeatedly scans the horizon for possible dangers. His companion says:
>
> (6) I really appreciate cautious drivers.
>
> > (Wilson 2006: 1726)

> A mother says to her teenage son:
>
> (7) I love children who keep their rooms clean,

58   3 IRONY AS ECHO

just as she has discovered that her son, once again, failed to clean his room.

(Gibbs & O'Brien 1991: 525)

These types of cases constitute an obstacle for Grice, as Wilson has noted (2006: 1726). However, an echoic account of these examples is not an easy task either.

Their formulation is ambiguous when we attempt to determine whether these cases should be accepted as instances in which the speaker is echoing a thought that she attributes to *someone other than herself at the current time*. It is likely true that in all these cases someone other than the speaker (as well as the speakers themselves at another time) believes that Danny knows a lot, appreciates cautious drivers or loves tidy children. However, in all the cases that we have analyzed thus far it appears that the utterance/thought echoed can be attributable to someone other than the speaker at the current time *but not to the speaker at the current time*.

This extreme is not clearly stated in the formulation of the echoic account and can be easily refuted. However, at least it would appear that there is a point to claiming that this is not the type of attribution that Sperber and Wilson were contemplating when they introduced the idea – why, otherwise, the need to specify that the attribution has to be directed to someone other than the speaker at the current time? If the stronger clause we deduced was not supposed to be intended, claiming that the echoed utterance/thought must be attributable to *someone* would be more than sufficient.

This is not the only problem that should concern the echoic account regarding this type of example. In addition to the instances of uncertain proper attribution, these cases are also problematic in that it is not easy to explain why the speaker should be assumed to be dissociating herself from the utterances/thoughts echoed. Wilson and Sperber certainly cannot claim that the aforementioned speakers are dissociating themselves from the attributive thoughts they are echoing because they are ludicrously false – because, as we have ascertained, in all cases the speaker believes the literal meaning of the utterance to be true. Thus, it must be that those three thoughts are 'blatantly inadequate in other ways' (Wilson & Sperber 2012: 130).

However, how is it inadequate to claim that someone knows a lot when we actually believe that he does know a lot? We cannot be referring here to the adequacy of this claim in terms of politeness or social expectations – in fact, it may be much more

3.3 *Some Developments*   59

adequate in this scenario for Jesse to have sincerely said that Danny knows a lot.

Arguably, Wilson and Sperber are attempting to explain that these speakers are not properly *saying* the literal meanings of their utterances – they are not intending to communicate what they would express if they uttered the same sentences literally. However, in their attempt to characterize this act of *not saying* the literal meaning of the utterance, the notions of attribution and dissociation are at least problematic, if not limited.

3.3 SOME DEVELOPMENTS

3.3.1 Echoic Reminder Theory

Roger J. Kreuz and Sam Glucksberg (1989) presented the 'echoic reminder theory' to explain verbal irony. This account is generally viewed as a revision of Sperber and Wilson's echoic theory but also as a variant of the so-called pretence theories of irony. In fact, these authors aimed at providing an account of irony that overcomes the limitations of both the pretence and echoic approaches.

It is clear that Kreuz and Glucksberg favour the one-stage view of irony postulated by the pretence and echoic accounts, in contrast to the opposition-based two-stage view promoted by the classical Gricean approaches. This classical account, they claim, does not touch on the most interesting aspects of irony.

These authors acknowledge that the reminder function of ironic statements was alluded to in Sperber and Wilson's theory. In the echoic account, ironic utterances are echoic interpretations, but the central point to emphasize would be that such echoes aim at *reminding* the hearer of an existing expectation (either implicit or explicit). This is why Kreuz and Glucksberg claim that the theory should be renamed the 'echoic reminder theory'. They say that their account is perfectly consistent with the echoic account of irony but that the latter is to a certain extent incomplete.

Aside from the terminological issue, Kreuz and Glucksberg maintain that the idea of reminder is more general than echo, and hence it can be applied to a wider variety of ironic instances. They consider an utterance to be echoic when it alludes to a previous event or antecedent. A reminder can occur, they state, even if the utterance does not allude to an actual antecedent. Thus, according to these authors, echoic interpretation would be a particular case of a reminder.

60   3 IRONY AS ECHO

One advantage of this view is that it can explain the asymmetry issue of irony, that is, the question of why irony is typically negative and rarely positive. What these authors claim is essentially that positive irony requires an explicit antecedent, unlike regular negative irony. This is so because the implicit norms we typically share tend to be positive, and these can work as easily graspable antecedents for negative ironic utterances. The requirement of having an explicit antecedent therefore would make positive irony more complex and thus scarcer.

> Implicit reminding, therefore, is sufficient for positive statements intended ironically because there are positive norms to be reminded of. In contrast, implicit reminding should not be sufficient for negative statements intended ironically because normally there are no implicit negative norms to be reminded of. (Kreuz & Glucksberg 1989: 376)

Another benefit of this approach is that it can explain certain ironic cases that are problematic for the echoic account. Kreuz and Glucksberg note that the distinction between use and mention on which the first version of the echoic theory was based can certainly account for cases of irony in which the literal meaning of the utterance is not intended but not for those cases in which the speaker may intend the literal meaning of her utterance. They present the following example:

> (22) Would you very much mind if I asked you, please, to perhaps consider cleaning up your room sometime this month?
>
> (Kreuz & Glucksberg 1989: 383)

Kreuz and Glucksberg claim that in this case the speaker is *using* the utterance to make a request (even if ironically), instead of *mentioning* it. This cannot be a case of an echoic mention then. It is certainly a case of a reminder, however; it recalls the speaker's attitude towards the hearer's behaviour.

This is not the only issue where the echoic reminder theory may overtake Sperber and Wilson's account. Kreuz and Glucksberg recall the case of Jonathan Swift's *A Modest Proposal*, an essay that cannot be considered an echoic mention but that can easily be understood in terms of pretence or reminder. They join with Clark and Gerrig here and acknowledge that the pretence theory is, at least in certain aspects, more powerful than the echoic account. However, ultimately, the echoic reminder theory is also more suitable than the pretence theory. In fact, Kreuz and Glucksberg claim that Clark and Gerrig's theory is overly general, as it can be applied to all indirect speech.

3.3 Some Developments

Therefore, the echoic reminder theory should be accepted as a correction and development of both the echoic and pretence approaches to irony (which Kreuz and Glucksberg in fact claim do not differ from one another significantly).

The echoic reminder theory has been viewed as an interesting contribution to the pragmatics of irony, as it introduced the valuable idea of the reminding nature of irony and particularly in that it offered experimental data contributing to the debate on positive irony. Overall, it has not been embraced as a suitable alternative to the echoic theory (Attardo 2000: 809; Wilson & Sperber 2012: 125), as it is considered to have inherited the same limitations while not offering significant improvements to the original conception of echo. Several difficulties that Kreuz and Glucksberg signalled with regard to the echoic mention view of irony were overcome with the development of this theory[2] but with no need of introducing the idea of reminder.

3.3.2 Curcó's Proposal

The echoic account of irony has many adepts who have developed the account's basic ideas and presented counter-arguments to other theories' criticisms. Carmen Curcó has defended the echoic account of irony, particularly from the charges directed against this view by Giora and her indirect negation conception of irony.

Curcó takes into consideration Giora's criticisms of the view of irony defended by relevance theory. Giora purported that irony does not have to be echoic, as the following examples allegedly show:

Said on a very rainy day:

(23) I think the washing hasn't dried.

(Giora 1995: 246)

'Do you know any G.M.?', my friend asks.

(24) 'Rings a bell', I reply (given that the person in question is well known to the speakers).

(Giora 1995: 246)

---

[2] We should bear in mind that what Kreuz and Glucksberg are criticizing is the first stage of development of the echoic theory, where irony is explained in terms of echoic mentions. We have already observed that this theory developed quickly over the years and abandoned the idea of mention in favour of that of interpretation initially and then of the idea of attribution.

62   3 IRONY AS ECHO

The problem for the echoic account, Giora claims, is that utterances
(23) and **(24)** need not be attributed to another speaker, although they
are instances of irony. However, she considers attribution to be
a necessary condition in terms of relevance theory, hence its inability
to explain such cases.

Curcó is prepared to accept that Giora may be correct to a certain
extent. Utterances **(23)** and **(24)** may not be attributable to someone
other than the speaker. However, Curcó considers that Giora neglects
certain features of the echoic account and that her arguments are lacking
in this respect. Regarding the case of these supposedly non-echoic ironic
utterances, Curcó argues that the definition of echo does not assume that
the speaker must echo a belief she attributes to someone else.

Giora considers that with this, Curcó expands on Sperber and
Wilson's echoic account (Giora 1998: 5), while Curcó herself considers
that Giora's initial arguments regarding the non-attributiveness of
certain cases was itself based on a misinterpretation of the relevantist
idea of interpretive use (Curcó 2000: 262).

Giora's second criticism purports that there are echoes accompanied by ridicule that are nevertheless not ironic cases (Giora 1995:
248). This would show, she claims, that an echo and a dissociative
attitude are not sufficient elements to delimit irony. She is thinking of
the following type of case:

> DINA: I missed the last news broadcast. What did the Prime Minister
>   say about the Palestinians?
> MIRA (with ridiculing aversion):
>
> (25) That we should deport them.
>
> (Giora 1995: 248)

Again, Curcó considers that Giora is misinterpreting the predictions of Sperber and Wilson's echoic account. She claims that
utterance **(25)** fails to be an interpretive use of language, as the
utterance is clearly used descriptively in this context. It should not
surprise us, therefore, that it fails to be an ironic case as well.
As Curcó claims,

> It would be very strange for a theory to predict that any case of
> reported speech combined with the implicit expression of a
> dissociative attitude on the part of the speaker would produce an
> instance of verbal irony, and certainly this is not what Sperber and
> Wilson's characterization of irony does.
>   It therefore seems that Giora's objections to the relevance theoretic
> approach to irony are unfounded. (Curcó 2000: 263)

3.4 SUMMARY

Sperber and Wilson's relevance theory is a sound theory of communication, including when applied to the analysis of irony. The echoic account of irony has two strong points. It is the first theory that offers a strong alternative to the classical pragmatic account of irony. In addition, it is a fully developed theory, robust and stable, and it has touched on almost every aspect concerning ironic communication.

Whether it is truly the alternative to the classical Gricean account, that is, whether it explains ironic communication more adequately than its predecessor, is an issue that remains open. The truth is that supporters are not lacking on either side, and new arguments continue to be presented in favour of both the echoic and the opposition views of irony.

Because it has touched on so many aspects concerning irony, there are a considerable number of issues upon which the echoic account is in disagreement with another approach. In addition to the traditional confrontation with the Gricean view, the other main challengers to Sperber and Wilson in the realm of irony are the pretence-based approaches. In Chapter 4, I focus on these accounts of irony and consider how they are positioned on the general map of the pragmatics of irony.

3.5 SUGGESTED READING

3.5.1 Sperber and Wilson

The originators of the echoic account have devoted several works to the analysis of irony:

Sperber, D. 1984. Verbal irony: pretense or echoic mention? *Journal of Experimental Psychology: General* 113(1): 130–436.

Sperber, D. & D. Wilson. 1981. Irony and the use-mention distinction. In *Radical Pragmatics*, ed. P. Cole, 295–318. New York: Academic Press.

Sperber, D. & D. Wilson. 1986/95. *Relevance: Communication and Cognition.* Oxford: Blackwell.

Sperber, D. & D. Wilson. 1998. Irony and relevance: a reply to Seto, Hamamoto and Yamanashi. In *Relevance Theory: Applications and Implications*, ed. R. Carston & S. Uchida, 283–93. Amsterdam: John Benjamins.

Wilson, D. 2006. The pragmatics of verbal irony: echo or pretense? *Lingua* 116: 1722–43.

Wilson, D. 2009. Irony and metarepresentation. *UCL Working Papers in Linguistics* 21: 183–226.

Wilson, D. 2013. Irony comprehension: a developmental perspective. *Journal of Pragmatics* 59: 40–56.

Wilson, D. & D. Sperber. 1992. On verbal irony. *Lingua* 87: 53–76.

Wilson, D. & D. Sperber. 2012. *Meaning and Relevance.* Cambridge: Cambridge University Press.

3.5.2 Criticisms of the Echoic Account

Many authors have criticized the echoic account from different perspectives. The following chapter by Ken-ichi Seto examines the concept of echo and signals its limitations and strong points:

Seto, K. 1998. On non-echoic irony. In *Relevance Theory: Applications and Implications,* ed. R. Carston & S. Uchida, 239–55. Amsterdam: John Benjamins.

The following three authors touch on the weak aspects of the echoic approach and defend different version of classical (neo-)Gricean theories of irony:

Camp, E. 2012. Sarcasm, pretense, and the semantics/pragmatics distinction. *Noûs* 46(4): 587–634.

Garmendia, J. 2015. A (neo-)Gricean account of irony: an answer to relevance theory. *International Review of Pragmatics* 7: 40–79.

Giora, R. 1995. On irony and negation. *Discourse Processes* 19: 239–64.

3.5.3 Some Developments

For further details on authors that develop the idea of echo, the following works may be useful:

Curcó, C. 2000. Irony: negation, echo and metarepresentation. *Lingua* 110: 257–80.

Kreuz, R. J. & S. Glucksberg. 1989. How to be sarcastic: the echoic reminder theory of verbal irony. *Journal of Experimental Psychology: General* 118(4): 374–86.

Yus, F. 2000. On reaching the intended ironic interpretation. *International Journal of Communication* 10(1–2): 27–78.

4 Irony as Pretence

Irony is related to the notion of pretence in several ways. Dramatic irony, for instance, is a particular ironic manifestation used in ancient Greek theatre, from which the name of irony arose, as I have already explained. Thus, we can state that irony was, to a certain extent, conceived on the stage.

However, here we are concerned with verbal irony within natural conversation, and therefore, we are outside any stage or theatrical scenario. We have noted that the Gricean account was the first pragmatic explanation of irony and that the echoic account was subsequently presented as an alternative. The 'pretence theory' of irony, as postulated by Herbert Clark and Richard Gerrig (1984), may be viewed as an alternative to both the Gricean and the echoic approaches. It is typically considered to be closer to the echoic view, as they both agree that there is only one meaning in irony, in contrast to (neo-)Gricean approaches, which defend the idea of irony as a two-stage phenomenon. However, its seed can be found in Grice's approach, as Grice had mentioned in his brief notes that being ironic is to a certain extent related to pretending.

Several theories followed this thread opened up by Grice and developed explanations of verbal irony based on the notion of pretence. The first and probably among the most influential is Clark and Gerrig's pretence theory of irony. In the following sections, I will explain its basic claims (4.1) and its limitations and difficulties (4.2). In Section 4.3, I will compare the echoic and pretence views of irony. Subsequently, in Section 4.4, I will consider several other pretence-based accounts that diverge from Clark and Gerrig's in different ways.

4.1 THE PRETENCE THEORY

Clark and Gerrig's pretence theory of irony is typically viewed as being close to the echoic account of irony to the extent that both are

66   4 IRONY AS PRETENCE

positioned in favour of a single-stage view of irony and at odds with
the classical Gricean view, which posits two opposite meanings in
irony. The pretence and echoic theories have even been considered
to be indistinguishable from each other in that a speaker who can be
viewed as echoing an utterance/thought could also be viewed as
pretending to be someone who uttered/thought so. Authors from
both sides strive to demonstrate that echo and pretence are two
different notions and that they result in different explanations of
ironic communication. Some defend the echoic view and deny that
pretence is required for irony, whereas others postulate that it is
pretence and not echo that we find in every ironic utterance. I will
focus on this debate in Section 4.3.

Despite the proximity between the echoic and pretence accounts
and their apparent estrangement from the classical approach, Clark
and Gerrig present their theory as a direct descendant of Grice's view
of irony. In fact, the work in which they introduce their theory (Clark
& Gerrig 1984) starts with a defence of Grice from the attacks of the
echoic view and aims to demonstrate that his direction (refined in
their own pretence account), and not the echoic one, is the right
course for a pragmatic explanation of irony.

Grice did mention that ironic speakers pretend, and thus, according
to Clark and Gerrig, he linked his account to long-standing ideas on
irony originating as far back as the ancient Greek era.

> To be ironical is, among other things, to pretend (as the etymology
> suggests), and while one wants the pretense to be recognized as such, to
> announce it as a pretense would spoil the effect. (Grice 1967b/89: 54)

Thus, the pretence theory should be seen as an attempt to expand on
Grice's notes such that the superiority of Grice's position is
manifested.

From Grice, Clark and Gerrig adopt the view of the ironic speaker as
not *saying* or *using* a proposition but, instead, pretending to use it. They
emphasize this point, as they consider that the Gricean approach has
been misunderstood in this respect. In fact, when attempting to show
that Grice's approach to irony is inadequate, it is common to assume
that for Grice the ironic speaker *uses* a literal meaning that is opposite
to the one she actually intends to communicate.[1] This would be in
complete disagreement with the echoic account, which claimed in the
first stage of the theory that the ironic speaker does not use
a proposition but mentions it. What Clark and Gerrig claim is that it

---

[1] See, for example, Jorgensen et al. (1984).

4.1 The Pretence Theory

is erroneous to confront Grice and Sperber and Wilson on this issue. Grice clearly stated that the ironic speaker pretends, and we should thus understand that the speaker, when being ironic, *pretends to use* a proposition instead of truly using it.

In addition to the influence of Grice, Clark and Gerrig acknowledge Henry W. Fowler's influence on their account, particularly with regard to the idea of a double audience. Fowler, in his *Dictionary of Modern English Usage*, defined irony in the following way:

> Irony is a form of utterance that postulates a double audience, consisting of one party that hearing shall hear and shall not understand, and another party that, when more is meant than meets the ear, is aware both of that more and of the outsiders' incomprehension. [It] may be denned as the use of words intended to convey one meaning to the uninitiated part of the audience and another to the initiated, the delight of it lying in the secret intimacy set up between the latter and the speaker. (Fowler 1965: 305–6, quoted in Clark & Gerrig 1984: 121–22)

Fowler's contribution, along with Grice's notes on the pretending nature of irony, leads to Clark and Gerrig's pretence theory. When being ironic, then, a speaker pretends to be someone addressing an unknowing audience; the hearer is expected to understand that the speaker is pretending and that she intends to mock either someone who may utter the sentence sincerely (the pretended speaker), someone who may accept what the speaker is pretending to say (the pretended audience), or the utterance itself.

The notion of the double audience leads to another idea that is worth noting here: the hearer, when processing an ironic utterance, must recognize the speaker's pretence and the fact that the speaker is mocking the hearers who do not (or would not) see through the pretence – the imagined audience. This binds together speaker and hearer, as it creates what Fowler calls a 'secret intimacy'. According to Clark and Gerrig, this is the aspect of irony that delights the hearer and would explain the use of irony itself as a mechanism creating a bond between speakers and hearers.

The double audience creates two distinct types of victims of irony as well. One is the person who the speaker is pretending to be (the pretended speaker), as the speaker may well be ridiculing her. The other type includes the members of the audience who do not (or would not) recognize that the speaker is pretending, as the speaker may also mock their ignorance. These victims can be a specific person or a recognizable type of person.

68   4 IRONY AS PRETENCE

The sum of these features constitutes the basics of the pretence theory
of irony, which Clark and Gerrig summarize in the following manner:

> Suppose S is speaking to A, the primary addressee, and to A', who may
> be present or absent, real or imaginary. In speaking ironically, S is
> pretending to be S' speaking to A'. What S' is saying is, in one way or
> another, patently uni[n]formed or injudicious, worthy of a 'hostile or
> derogatory judgment or a feeling such as indignation or contempt'
> (Grice 1978: 124). A' in ignorance, is intended to miss this pretence, to
> take S as speaking sincerely. But A, as part of the 'inner circle' (to use
> Fowler's phrase), is intended to see everything – the pretence, S's
> injudiciousness, A's ignorance, and hence S's attitude toward S', A',
> and what S' said. (Clark & Gerrig 1984: 122)

Thus described, this account appears applicable to the variety of
ironic examples we have considered thus far.

> X, with whom A has been on close terms until now, has betrayed a secret
> of A's to a business rival. A and his audience both know this. A says:
>
> (3) X is a fine friend.
>
> (Grice 1967a/89: 34)

In Grice's example, A would be pretending to be someone who
truly considers that X is a fine friend (maybe A himself in a previous
time), speaking to someone who does not know that X betrayed
A (someone who may actually be present at the time of the utterance
or not). What the pretended speaker is saying, that X is a fine friend,
does not sound reasonable, as both speaker and hearer know that
X betrayed A. The idea that X is a fine friend is thus worthy of
indignation. Someone who is not aware of X's betrayal will not
recognize that A is pretending and being ironic, but the informed
hearer will recognize the pretence, the irony and the attitude A is
attempting to convey. Finally, this game of recognizing actual and
pretended sayings and attitudes will create an intimate bond
between speaker and hearer.

The examples that were problematic for Grice because no opposition was involved do not appear to be an issue for the pretence theory.

> During the precept, Danny was dominating the discussion. He
> certainly seemed to be familiar with the subject, but he was obnoxious
> in the way he showed off his knowledge. Jesse, one of Danny's
> classmates, said:
>
> (5) You sure know a lot.
>
> (Kumon-Namakura et al. 1995: 7)

4.1 The Pretence Theory 69

It appears to make suitable sense of the utterance to claim that Jesse is pretending to be someone who actually wants to praise Danny. Those who agree that Danny has shown a pretentious attitude (and hence does not deserve to be praised currently) will recognize that Jesse is pretending to say these words while ridiculing Danny, his attitude and anyone who may believe that he is worthy of praise.

Clearly, echoic irony also fits within the pretence approach, if only because the echo helps the pretence be more easily recognizable.

> PETER: It's a lovely day for a picnic.

> They go for a picnic and it rains.

> MARY (sarcastically):

> (15) It's a lovely day for a picnic, indeed.

> (Sperber & Wilson 1986/95: 239)

Mary, as she is repeating Peter's words and thus clearly echoing his utterance, is definitely pretending to be Peter talking seriously about the weather. Her mocking attitude is directed at him, as he will be the main victim of her irony. Peter will probably not miss Mary's pretence, as she is echoing his previous words, and he will immediately recognize her intentions to mock him and his predictions.

Activity 4.1 Pretence Theory

It is time to revisit your irony samples and use them to verify the claims of Clark and Gerrig's pretence theory. Try to answer the following questions regarding your examples. Again, you can see the replies for my own sample below.

1. Would you say that the speaker is pretending to be someone else? Who is S'?
2. Are there two distinguishable audiences in the example (A, who is expected to understand the irony, and A', who will miss it)?
3. Does what S' is saying deserve a 'hostile or derogatory judgement'?

Discussion

(0)   That was a clumsy woman driving.

1. *Yes*. It appears that in this case the speaker, Maia, would be pretending to be the addressee, Ku. Thus, Ku would be S'.

> 2. Not in this case. Ku is the only hearer, and he will (and is expected to) recognize the pretence and the irony. Ku is A.
>
>   Nevertheless, we can imagine that someone else is in the scenario; let us call her Queen. If Queen does not know that Ku typically blames women for driving badly and that Maia always confronts Ku on this issue, then maybe Queen will miss the irony here: she may believe that Maia mistook the male driver for a woman, for example. In this case, Queen would miss the pretence, the attitude and the irony. Queen is A'.
>
> 3. *Yes.* It deserves a derogatory judgement, at least in terms of the speaker, as she believes that it is nonsense to link someone's driving skills to her gender.

Thus far, those are the basics of ironic communication in terms of the pretence theory. However, Clark and Gerrig also touched on the three aspects of irony that were central in Grice's account and the echoic theory.

(i) Irony Can Also Be Positive

Clark and Gerrig openly acknowledge that positive irony does exist and that there is an asymmetry between positive and negative irony – the former is scarcer than the latter. They claim that the pretence theory can adequately explain this imbalance. In fact, following Jorgensen et al. (1984), they assume that we typically understand the world based on ideas of success and excellence. Moreover, people in ignorance may hold on to these positive ideas particularly tightly. As this is the type of people the ironic speaker typically pretends to be, it should not surprise us that speakers when being ironic tend to engage in more positive pretences than negative ones.

> #### Pollyanna, the Optimistic Child
>
> *Pollyanna* is a novel for children written by American novelist Eleanor H. Porter in 1913. The main character of the story is a young orphan named *Pollyanna*, who must adjust to a new life at her strict aunt Polly's wealthy home. Despite all the difficulties she confronts, Pollyanna always looks at the bright side of things and plays the 'Glad Game', as her father taught her. This game essentially consists in finding something to be glad about in every situation, always displaying a positive attitude.

4.2 Problems

> The novel had great success and soon became widely renowned, to the extent that people who show an unrestrained optimism are often characterized as 'Pollyannaish'. Those who follow Pollyanna's philosophy of life are essentially people who focus on the positive aspects of life.
>
> On the academic level, Boucher and Osgood (1969) presented what they called the 'Pollyanna hypothesis'. In line with several prior findings, they found empirical evidence that people tend to use positively evaluative words more frequently than negatively evaluative ones. Clark and Gerrig (1984) pick up this thread to explain the asymmetry of evaluation in irony, which is due, they claim, to people's tendency to view the world as Pollyanna did, focusing on the bright side of life.

(ii) To Speak Ironically Is to Pretend

Clark and Gerrig claim that the ironic speaker pretends and that it is this pretence that ties together every instance of irony. This position initiated a dispute with the advocates of the echoic theory. I focus on this in Section 4.3.

(iii) Ironic Speaker's Tone of Voice

We have noted that Grice was not conclusive regarding the ironic speaker's tone of voice: it appears that she may use a tone connected with the attitude she is conveying. Sperber and Wilson essentially agree with Grice: the tone that speakers use when being ironic is connected to the dissociative attitude expressed when being ironic.

Clark and Gerrig's position appears different, although they acknowledge Grice's influence in this case as well. According to them, a speaker pretending to be someone else would abandon her own voice and adopt the voice corresponding to the person she is pretending to be. She may also exaggerate or caricaturize this voice. These authors claim that this would be a natural explanation of the alleged ironic speaker's tone of voice in terms of the pretence theory.

4.2 PROBLEMS

The pretence theory captures a classical feature of ironic communication – the ironic speaker has often been considered to be pretending, to be showing a false ignorance. However, the notion of pretence itself rapidly becomes problematic in this approach.

72   4 IRONY AS PRETENCE

Pretence is not clearly distinguished from make-believe, making as if, acting, insincerity, and many other non-ironic manifestations. Clark and Gerrig's pretence theory has trouble overcoming this general conception of pretence and risks confusing ironic and non-ironic discourse.

Moreover, in Clark and Gerrig's explanation of irony, it appears that two different ideas of pretence may be combined. First, they continually refer to Grice's account when explaining their own, particularly when discussing the notion of pretence. On these occasions, it appears that pretending is considered to be something very close to Grice's idea of making as if to say: it is 'not saying' a literal meaning but employing it in a certain way in order to communicate ironic content. It is also in this sense that pretence is understood when they claim, responding to the echoic account, that the ironic speaker does not properly *use* a proposition (within the use-mention dichotomy the other approach proposes).

This first conception of pretence could be viewed as a *weak use* of the term. It aims to characterize what ironic speakers do when uttering a sentence ironically, as they do not *say* or *use words* in the proper sense. However, the truth is that instead of properly explaining what it is that these ironic speakers do instead, Clark and Gerrig just put forward what it is that they do not do – ironic speakers do not use a proposition; they do not say the literal meaning. This first conception of pretence appears to concur with Grice's and neo-Gricean explanations of irony. However, apart from the terminological issue (what has been called 'to make as if to say' could easily be called 'to pretend'), Clark and Gerrig's account of pretence does not add any specification regarding what this act of *not saying* consists of.

In addition to Grice's position, Clark and Gerrig employ several other ideas when characterizing the act of pretending. First, they mention that the ignorant audience will deem the speaker to be speaking sincerely – thus, it appears that the ironic speaker is not sincere. Second, quoting Ryle (1950), they compare the ironic speaker's pretending with actors' acting:

> Actors in speaking their parts before the audience are not, strictly, using their words. They are not being defiant, remorseful, loving, or desperate, but only pretending to be so. Their utterances cannot be classified as either 'use' or 'mention' (p. 339). (Clark & Gerrig 1984: 23)

Thus, a speaker when being ironic does not use words, just as actors do not use words when acting. Third, in certain occasions they equate the

4.3 Pretence versus Echo 73

ideas of pretence and make-believe, and they lead us to Kendall Walton's works for a complete characterization of both.

These three branches of influence (insincerity, acting and make-believe), instead of bolstering the weak conception of pretence, undermine it. Insincerity may be related to irony to a certain extent, but they are not the same thing, and claiming that the ironic speaker is insincere will not help to delimitate the idea of pretending without further specifications. Indeed, lies are the most paradigmatic case of insincerity, but being ironic is not the same as lying.

Make-believe can also be viewed as related to pretence, but this notion is broad and general, and it is applicable to many instances other than ironic ones. Children when playing can be observed using make-believe, although no irony may be found in these games. Thus, to link irony to these two related notions without clearly stating which differences apply to them does not help strengthen the characterization of pretence.

The case of acting is even more complex. It may be true that actors do not, properly speaking, use their words and that ironic speakers do not use their words either – but they 'do not use their words' in a different way. Actors on stage speak within the realm of fiction, and their discourse follows the rules of fictional speech. Irony does not. Irony can be used either in fictional or non-fictional discourse, but the use of irony itself does not place the speaker in a fictional setting.

The ideas of make-believe or acting may be connected to irony in a different way. Clark and Gerrig claim that the ironic speaker abandons her own voice and adopts someone else's voice. Claiming that the speaker is thus acting or making believe in that she is demonstrating that she is not strictly using her words makes sense. If this is the sense in which the ironic speaker should be considered to be pretending, then a different and *stronger sense* of pretence is in play. Ironic speakers act, make believe or pretend as a way of demonstrating that they should be understood ironically. However, that notion of pretence does not correspond to the idea of 'not saying' that we find in every ironic instance but to a strategy that the ironic speaker uses on certain occasions. I shall return to this strong characterization of pretence in Chapter 6 when I focus on the clues that ironic speakers often employ.

4.3 PRETENCE VERSUS ECHO

Clark and Gerrig devote most of their 1984 paper to signalling the advantages of their approach compared with Sperber and Wilson's

74 4 IRONY AS PRETENCE

echoic theory.[2] The criticisms the echoic account directs towards Grice's view of irony are, according to Clark and Gerrig, unfounded, and thus a Gricean inspired theory, as the pretence theory is claimed to be, can address the peculiarities of irony adequately.

Sperber and Wilson interpret, still according to Clark and Gerrig, that Grice assumes that the ironic speaker *uses* the words she utters. This would lead us to a problematic view of irony – by now we know very well that a speaker cannot be considered as *saying* when being ironic, hence neither as properly *using* her words. Thus, Sperber and Wilson's explanation of irony in terms of echoic mention was presented as a solution to this problem that Grice would face.

Clark and Gerrig clarify two points here. First, it is not true that Grice assumed that ironic speakers use the words they utter, which is why he explained that speakers pretend when being ironic. However, if there were a problem in Grice's account, a solution as valid as Sperber and Wilson's alternative would be to explain irony in terms of pretence.

Sperber and Wilson responded immediately. Sperber (1984) clarified that their interpretation of Grice's notes was far from being misinformed and was in no way original. He acknowledged that Grice mentioned that being ironic is to a certain extent related to pretending, but he claimed that 'Grice, however, does not attempt to develop a pretence theory of irony, and this might also be in deference to ancient wisdom' (Sperber 1984: 136).

Thus, it is here that the contest between echoists and pretenders arises.

4.3.1 In Favour of Pretence

Clark and Gerrig state that every echoic irony can be reinterpreted as a case of pretence, whereas not every irony that is easily explainable in terms of pretence can be viewed as an echo (Clark & Gerrig 1984: 123). The consequence is clear: pretence is a more suitable notion for explaining different types of ironic utterances.

Jonathan Swift's *A Modest Proposal* – a 1729 essay in which the author suggests that poor Irish families should sell their children as food to the rich to ease their economic troubles – would be an example of this. This essay is considered to be entirely ironic, from beginning to end.

---

[2] It should be noted that Clark and Gerrig's paper on the pretence theory of irony was published in 1984. They are thus considering the echoic theory in its first developmental stage, when irony was considered to be an echoic mention (in terms of the mention/use distinction). See Section 3.1. for further details.

4.3 *Pretence versus Echo* 75

Sperber and Wilson's only option would thus be to maintain that the entire essay is an echoic mention. However, that would be the wrong alternative to follow. According to Clark and Gerrig, the irony in *A Modest Proposal* works precisely because it is impossible that anyone could ever have entertained its arguments seriously. This makes it impossible for the irony to be echoic, as it is impossible for anything to be echoed behind this essay.

In contrast, a pretence-based account of Swift's essay works perfectly well. Swift – or maybe the narrator in Swift's essay – would be pretending to be an Englishman speaking to a rich audience. Applying Grice's idea of pretence and Fowler's concept of double audience, the pretence theory can explain how Swift intended his actual audience to recognize the pretence and, beyond it, to grasp what he was ironically communicating: a critical attitude towards Englishmen and particularly their disrespectful attitudes towards the poor Irish.

Clark and Gerrig anticipate an alternative direction that Sperber and Wilson could take on this issue. The echoic theory acknowledges that not every mention echoes an explicit source and that implicit echoes of shared opinions or popular wisdom are also common. This could be the case in Swift's essay: the writer could be echoing shared ideas or opinions with regard to the Irish, to Englishmen, and so on. Nevertheless, this would be the wrong direction to take, they claim. If the entire essay can be considered an implicit echo, then certainly anything can be considered as such. This is one of the significant weaknesses of the echoic theory according to Clark and Gerrig: it accepts that there may be implicit echoes, but it does not explain the conditions necessary for something to be accepted as such.

The pretence theory is again claimed to be safe from this limitation. Clark and Gerrig maintain that their theory clearly states what would count or not as a pretence.

> Ironists can pretend to use the words of any person or type of person they wish, just as long as they can get the intended audience to recognize the pretence and, thereby, their attitude toward the speaker, audience, and sentiment of that pretence. (Clark & Gerrig 1984: 24)

With this view on the issue, the pretence theory can explain both cases of explicit echoes and cases of non-echoic irony.

4.3.2 In Favour of Echo

Sperber (1984) answers Clark and Gerrig's charges and affirms that the picture is the exact opposite: it is the pretence theory that has

76   4 IRONY AS PRETENCE

problems explaining cases of irony for which the echoic view can account effortlessly.

The limitations that Clark and Gerrig believe they detect in the echoic theory derive from an erroneous conception that Clark and Gerrig have of Sperber and Wilson's claims. In fact, according to Sperber, Clark and Gerrig believe that the echoic theory claims that the source of an echo is always an existing utterance or otherwise a received opinion. However, Sperber asserts that this is a totally mistaken view of the theory. What the echoic theory predicts is that ironic utterances mention meanings that echo thoughts. These echoed thoughts must merely be attributable to a specific person, a type of person or to people in general (Sperber 1984: 132). Thus, the cases that Clark and Gerrig believe cannot be explained in terms of echo are easily explainable if we bear in mind the real notion of echo Sperber and Wilson put forward in their theory.

To the criticism that the echoic account does not clarify what the conditions are for accepting something as an echo, Sperber again has a ready answer. For an echo to be considered as such, he states, the distinctive criterion is that it be recognizable as an echo. According to Sperber, this is a perfectly efficient criterion if we bear in mind that when we recognize echoes, we are steeped in the game of verbal comprehension and thus follow the principle of relevance (or any such rules governing conversation that we may assume).

However, Sperber does not just defend his account from Clark and Gerrig's criticisms. He also claims that it is the pretence theory that truly has limitations when explaining verbal irony in its entirety. He states that the notion of pretence is stricter than that of echo, and thus, whenever we have a pretence, we automatically have an echo.

> If you can identify the (type of) person who the ironist pretends to be when he or she utters a certain proposition, a fortiori you can identify that proposition as one that could be entertained by some (type of) person. (Sperber 1984: 132)

Nevertheless, Sperber corrects himself immediately (Sperber 1984: 133) and accepts that there may be cases of pretence that cannot be interpreted as cases of echoic mention, as Clark and Gerrig maintain. However, he then asserts that the types of cases that are pretence but not echo are not cases of irony either, the reason being that the pretence theory cannot distinguish irony from certain neighbouring phenomena – parody, in particular.

4.3 *Pretence versus Echo* 77

Thus, when pretence is found *in an instance of irony*, then an echoic mention will also be found there. Furthermore, the reverse does not hold: echo will be found in certain cases of irony in which no pretence is detected. Sperber presents two types of examples that support this affirmation.

For instance, it is possible for an ironic speaker to echo a thought even if the person who entertained it (S', in Clark and Gerrig's terms) would never express it.

> Suppose Bill, who wants everybody to think of him as a totally sincere person, tells a transparent lie and believes he is believed. Judy says ironically,
>
> (26) What a clever lie!
>
> (Sperber 1984: 33)

In this example, Sperber notes, it makes no sense to claim that Judy is pretending to be Bill because Bill would never claim **(26)**. It appears adequate, however, to explain this case as Judy echoing a thought that Bill entertains but would never express.

Furthermore, there exist self-contradictory ironic utterances, such as the following:

> (27) Jones, this murderer, this thief, this crook, is indeed an honourable fellow!
>
> (Sperber 1984: 33)
>
> (28) Outside temperature is again below freezing point: a true heat wave!
>
> (Sperber 1984: 33)

Neither of these two cases can be explained in terms of pretence, as no speaker could have uttered either of these utterances non-ironically, and thus there is no one the speaker could pretend to be. Conversely, **(27)** and **(28)** can be explained if we consider that the speakers were mentioning a part of them – the meaning of 'honourable fellow' in **(27)** and 'a true heat wave' in **(28)**.

Thus, Clark and Gerrig hold that the pretence theory can explain all instances of irony, whereas the echoic account cannot, and Sperber affirms just the contrary: that echo is a suitable notion for explaining every ironic case, whereas pretence cannot be found in every irony. This may be the main and most difficult issue confronting the echoic and pretence views; however, there are several more specific aspects of irony that also enter into this debate between pairs.

78   4 IRONY AS PRETENCE

4.3.3 Types of Irony

According to Clark and Gerrig, another advantage of the pretence view is that it can explain the relationship between different types of irony. Following Fowler, Clark and Gerrig claim that what ties verbal irony, dramatic irony and irony of fate together is the existence of a double audience in the three of them. This is an element that the pretence theory properly introduces in the account, while the echoic account does not.

Sperber begins his 1984 paper by acknowledging that irony has been used to refer to many different things, but he settles the question straightforwardly, indirectly answering Clark and Gerrig by claiming that 'there may exist interesting relations among these referents, but there is no reason to expect all of them to fall under a single unified theory of irony' (Sperber 1984: 130).

4.3.4 Types of Victims

Thus, Sperber continues responding to every aspect Clark and Gerrig addressed in their work. According to the latter, the notion of a double audience also permits the pretence theory to distinguish between two types of victims: the injudicious speaker (S') and the ignorant audience (A'). The echoic account, as it lacks the distinction between audiences, cannot address this aspect either.

This is totally incorrect according to Sperber. He claims that not only does the pretence theory identify too many victims in irony, but moreover, they are not always the correct ones. An example of the first problem would be irony with no victims, as when someone utters

> (29) What lovely weather!
>
> (Sperber 1984: 134)

when the weather is actually miserable. The echoic account correctly predicts that there are no victims when universally shared ideas or norms are echoed. The pretence account, in contrast, will have a problem explaining how it is possible to be ironic without victimizing someone.

The second type of problem arises with irony that has several victims who do not properly fit within Clark and Gerrig's pair.

> Against Judy's advice, Bill bought what a crooked art dealer told him was a true Picasso. Roger, claiming to be competent, vouched for the painting's authenticity. Other friends of Bill's were much impressed by the painting until a genuine expert at last showed it to be a fake. When Judy then says,

4.4 Some Developments

(30) That was a truly beautiful Picasso!

(Sperber 1984: 134)

In this type of case, Sperber states, the echoic theory can discern any number of victims of different types, in contrast to the pretence theory, which predicts the presence of only two types of victims in each instance of irony.

4.3.5 The Speaker's Tone of Voice

Finally, Clark and Gerrig claim that a pretence-based account can best explain the role of the ironic speaker's tone of voice: a speaker, when being ironic, abandons her own voice and uses the voice corresponding to that of the speaker she is pretending to be (which she may also at times exaggerate). However, they are wrong in this respect as well, according to Sperber. Clark and Gerrig are mistaking the true ironic tone of voice with that of mimicking, and thus their predictions are inadequate. What Clark and Gerrig are describing in their account is in fact the tone of voice that corresponds to parody. In fact, Sperber claims that the very existence of the ironic speaker's tone of voice would contradict the claims of the pretence account because the presence of such a voice would make it impossible for an audience to miss the pretence, and it would thus be impossible for an ignorant audience to truly exist.

In subsequent works (Wilson 2006, 2013; Wilson & Sperber 2012), Sperber and Wilson have continued in the same vein, signalling the limitations of Clark and Gerrig's pretence theory and of certain theories they consider to be hybrid attributive-pretence accounts, which I shall introduce later. The bones of contention, however, remain the same.

4.4 SOME DEVELOPMENTS

Clark and Gerrig may have been the first to propose a pretence-based pragmatic characterization of irony, but they are not the only ones. In this section, I examine the most important pretence accounts of irony, including those which have attempted to refine the notion of pretence to explain irony as well as an approach that combines pretence with another feature to explain ironic communication.

4.4.1 Walton, Recanati and Currie

One of the difficulties of Clark and Gerrig's pretence theory of irony, as I have mentioned, is that the notion of pretence is not defined

80   4 IRONY AS PRETENCE

sufficiently concisely, although it is the core concept of the theory. Several other authors have also characterized irony in terms of pretence and attempted to shed light on this key notion.

Kendall Walton's work, Mimesis as Make-believe: On the Foundations of the Representational Arts (1990), focuses on analyzing works of fiction and representational works of art as cases of make-believe. It is in this context that he touches on non-literal uses of language, including irony. In his approach to verbal irony, he combines the notion of pretending with the expression of a ridiculing attitude, in line with the pretence-based accounts of irony. He states:

> This suggests a general account of irony (one variety of irony anyway) in terms of pretence. To speak ironically is to mimic or mock those one disagrees with, fictionally to assert what they do or might assert. Irony is sarcasm. One shows what it is like to make certain claims, hoping thereby to demonstrate how absurd or ridiculous it is to do so. (Walton 1990: 222)

Walton's idea of pretence is not far from Clark and Gerrig's, I would venture. To pretend, in irony, appears comparable to mimicking or 'fictionally asserting' while expressing a mocking or ridiculing attitude towards what (or whom) is pretended. For Walton, to pretend, in this sense, is to participate verbally in a game of make-believe.

In more recent work, Walton touched on the similarities and differences between irony and understatements and overstatements. He views irony as similar to understatement while more distant from overstatement (Walton 2017). It is in this context that he attempts to offer a general and basic characterization of irony (or of verbal irony in declarative sentences, as he specifies). He presents two possible alternatives: irony could be viewed as an utterance whose explicit content entails a salient contrast, or irony could be viewed as a case of echo, in line with Sperber and Wilson's theory.

Walton opts for the former alternative, which he believes can address the vast variety of ironic utterances, among which some will no doubt be cases of echoic irony. Utterances of verbal irony will thus make use of an explicit content which entails a contrast. The idea of contrast may appear to present Walton as adhering to Grice's contradiction-based account of irony. However, according to Walton, it is in terms of pretence that we should understand this salient contrast.

> To voice the salient contrast is easily regarded as pretending to assert what one means to deny, making as if to assert it. And at least when

4.4 Some Developments

> there is a recognizable target, the speaker might well use a sarcastic or mocking tone in so pretending, making fun of the idea she is rejecting. (Walton 2017: 117)

François Recanati also views irony as a case of pretence. According to Recanati, when a speaker speaks ironically, she 'does not really say, or at least she does not assert, what she "makes as if to say" (Grice's phrase)' (Recanati 2004: 71). Attempting to discern what this idea of *not saying* may mean, he notes that in ironic communication a key element is lacking: the force of a serious assertion.

Thus, an ironic speaker does not (seriously) assert what she puts forward. Instead, she 'plays someone else's part' or 'mimics an act of assertion', according to Recanati. Again, the idea of pretence appears related to that of mimicking or acting. Recanati adds a specification here, however.

> The act of assertion is precisely what the speaker does *not* perform when she says that *p* ironically; rather, she plays someone else's part and *mimics* an act of assertion accomplished by that person. She does so not by pretending that that person is speaking – if that were the case, 'I' would refer to that person under the pretense– but by herself endorsing the function of speaker and saying that p, while (i) not taking responsibility for what is being said, and (ii) implicitly ascribing that responsibility to someone else, namely the person whose act of assertion is being mimicked. (Recanati 2007: 220)

Recanati sides with Clark and Gerrig and holds that ironic speakers *merely* pretend to say or assert something. Nevertheless, to a certain extent, he appears to be advocating for a two-stage view of irony – a view that involves two different meanings in irony instead of a single meaning.

> By pretending to assert something, the speaker conveys something else, just as, in the other types of cases, by asserting something the speaker conveys something else. By pretending to say of Paul that he is a fine friend in a situation in which just the opposite is obviously true, the speaker manages to communicate that Paul is everything but a fine friend. (Recanati 2004: 71)

However, although Recanati may ostensibly appear to be thereby positioning himself alongside Grice and at odds with the echoic and pretence accounts, he clarifies that the mechanism underlying irony is not the inferential mechanism of implicatures (Recanati 2004: 48). The nature of that which is implied by pretending to assert something in irony is thus not very clear in Recanati's account. What he does specify is the double layering existing in the primary meaning of

82   4 IRONY AS PRETENCE

ironic utterances: we have a surface speech act that is pretended and an ironic act of staging the performance of that speech act (Recanati 2004: 77).

Gregory Currie is the third author developing the concept of pretence to apply it to ironic communication. Currie generally agrees with Clark and Gerrig's claims regarding irony and pretence and attempts to defend their position against Sperber and Wilson's criticisms. According to Currie, however, several details must be refined in Clark and Gerrig's pretence account to explain irony in all its variety.

Currie notes that when being ironic a speaker does not always pretend to be another person. Sperber and Wilson had previously noted this point, criticizing the pretence theory for not being able to explain cases such as **(26)** or this one:

> Imagine that Bill is prone to say of himself: 'I am a very patient person'. In response to a display of temper from Bill, Judy says, ironically:
>
> (31) Bill is such a patient person.
>
>   (Currie 2006: 119)

In this case, as advocates of the echoic theory claim, Judy cannot be considered as pretending to be Bill, as Bill himself would never say something like **(31)**. Currie accepts this limitation of the pretence theory as originally presented by Clark and Gerrig. In his view, the notion of pretence in irony would be better formulated in these terms:

> So what matters is that the ironist's utterance be an indication that he or she is pretending to have a limited or otherwise defective perspective, point of view, or stance, F, and in doing so puts us in mind of some perspective, point of view, or stance, G (which may be identical to F or merely resemble it) which is the target of the ironic comment. (Currie 2006: 118)

With this variation, Currie claims to have solved the problem detected in the original pretence account. In fact, in Bill and Judy's example, it would make sense to claim that Judy, when uttering **(31)**, is pretending to take a perspective according to which Bill is a patient person, and in so doing, she indicates that Bill actually believes that he is a patient person (even if he would not express such a belief with those exact words).

However, Sperber and Wilson detected other problems in the pretence theory as well. I have mentioned, for example, that

4.4 Some Developments

according to Sperber, Clark and Gerrig could not explain irony communicated via utterances that no one could ever utter seriously, such as the following:

> (27) Jones, this murderer, this thief, this crook, is indeed an honourable fellow!

> (Sperber 1984: 33)

In this type of case, if we admit that no one could assert the utterance seriously, then there appears to be no one who we could pretend to be when being ironic. Currie does not discern a problem here, however. He states that the important thing is not whether there exists a person whom we can pretend to be but whether we can pretend that such a person exists. With this view of the issue, utterances that involve a contradiction, such as **(27)**, could also be explained in terms of pretence: the speaker is not pretending to be a person who would seriously utter **(27)**; she is pretending that there may exist a person who could seriously utter **(27)**.

Currie aims to defend the pretence view against the echoic account of irony. He claims that even in the cases where an echo appears clearly identifiable, the irony can (and should) be understood in terms of pretence. He considers Sperber and Wilson's original example:

> PETER: It's a lovely day for a picnic.

> They go for a picnic and it rains.

> MARY (sarcastically):

> (15) It's a lovely day for a picnic, indeed.

> (Sperber & Wilson 1986/95: 239)

Here, claims Currie, Mary's utterance **(15)** is best explained as a case of pretence. At least, this is the most intuitive interpretation of what is occurring in Mary and Peter's dialogue, which is something that a proper theory should take into account.

> The answer is that, intuitively, such an exchange seems awfully like pretense; Peter and Mary seem to be making up a playful dialogue full of sayings to which they are manifestly not committed. Calling this pretense is very natural, and would hardly be objected to by anyone untouched by this debate. At the very least, we are owed an account of why this is not, contrary to appearances, pretense. (Currie 2006: 126)

84   4 IRONY AS PRETENCE

4.4.2 The Allusional Pretence Theory

Sachi Kumon-Nakamura, Sam Glucksberg and Mary Brown (1995) propose the 'allusional pretence theory' of discourse irony. This account may be considered a hybrid theory that adds the notion of allusion to that of pretending. Thus, their theory aims to amend the deficits of both echoic and contradiction-based theories of irony.

According to these authors, the traditional pragmatic theories of irony have difficulties explaining different types of cases. They present the following examples:

> Consider a situation in which two people approach a door. The first person to reach the door opens it and lets it swing shut behind her. The second person, carrying a heavy box, says,
>
> (32) Don't hold the door open. I'll just say 'open sesame'
>
> or
>
> (33) Thanks for holding the door.
>
> (Kumon-Nakamura et al. 1995: 4)

These two utterances count as ironic in the given situation. Nevertheless, they pose serious problems for Grice's view of irony and for the traditional pragmatic explanation of irony in general. One of the problems is identified in utterance **(33)**: the idea of the opposite meaning is not applicable to utterances other than declaratives. Furthermore, the Gricean approach cannot account for cases in which true assertions are used ironically (as in example **(5)** 'You sure know a lot', which we have already analyzed), and it does not explain why someone would say the opposite of what she means. These would be Grice's limitations according to Kumon-Nakamura et al.

Sperber and Wilson's echoic theory also encounters problems, according to these authors. The view of irony as echoic may explain certain cases of irony but not all of them. It cannot easily explain the following, for instance:

Questions

(34)   How old did you say you were?

> said to someone acting inappropriately for his or her age.
>
> (Kumon-Nakamura et al. 1995: 4)

Offerings

(35)   How about another small slice of pizza?

4.4 Some Developments

to someone who has just gobbled up the whole pie.

(Kumon-Nakamura et al. 1995: 4)

Over-Polite Requests

(36) Would you mind very much if I asked you to consider cleaning up your room sometime this year?

to an inconsiderate and slovenly housemate.

(Kumon-Nakamura et al. 1995: 4–5)

According to Kumon-Nakamura et al., these three instances of irony do not appear to be echoic. Instead, they all allude to expectations or norms that have been violated. In this sense, echoic utterances would be a type of allusive utterance. Irony can be echoic, but it is not necessarily so. In contrast, allusion is a necessary element of discourse irony. Every irony alludes to a prior prediction, expectation, preference or norm that has been violated. It is at this level that we will find a discrepancy in irony between what is expected and what actually is.

Thus, the allusional pretence theory claims to be more general and inclusive than the echoic theory. Instead of the notion of echo, Kumon-Nakamura et al. proclaim that it is allusion that we will find in every irony. However, they also claim to be more general than Grice's view. They assert that ironic utterances, rather than flouting Grice's maxim of quality, are pragmatically insincere. They use the term 'pretence' to refer to pragmatic insincerity, and this is how they include this notion in their theory, which is thus a hybrid theory that includes both echo and pretence.

Using the idea of pragmatic insincerity, this theory aims to explain two types of irony that were problematic for Grice. Indeed, true ironic statements can be pragmatically insincere. For instance, it is pragmatically insincere for a compliment to say 'you sure know a lot' to someone who has behaved arrogantly. In addition, pragmatic insincerity can be applied to utterances other than declaratives. Ironic utterances would then violate a felicity condition of speech acts: the speaker in utterance **(34)** does not want to know the answer to her question; **(35)** is an insincere offer because the speaker does not expect the hearer to accept it. Utterance **(36)** would also be pragmatically insincere, to the extent that '[t]he person making the request does not intend the excessive politeness, but instead uses over-polite language in order to express an attitude of irritation toward the recipient of the request' (Kumon-Nakamura et al. 1995: 5).

86 4 IRONY AS PRETENCE

The idea of pragmatic insincerity, along with the notion of allusion, allows us to explain every type of irony, according to Kumon-Nakamura et al. Their account is, they claim, a significant extension and elaboration of the existing pragmatic theories of irony: allusion is a broader and more general notion than Sperber and Wilson's echoic mention/interpretation and Kreuz and Glucksberg's echoic reminder, whereas pragmatic insincerity is an extension of Grice's flouting of the quality maxim or Clark and Gerrig's use of the term pretence.

4.5 SUMMARY

Irony has often been viewed as related to pretending, mimicking, make-believe or disguising. Clark and Gerrig attempted to place pretence at the core of irony and build a pragmatic characterization of ironic communication in terms of pretence.

The pretence theory scores a point in that it formalizes the idea of pretence in irony and gathers various related but dispersed elements. Examining irony from this perspective, we are able to touch on the speaker-hearer relationship, the different grades of victimization in irony, the importance of the speaker's tone of voice, and several other features of ironic communication.

The pretence theory attempts to gather different views on pretence, which may be viewed as a strength of this approach. However, this also constitutes the theory's weak point: the diverse ideas related to irony do not result in a united and consistent notion of pretence. A number of authors have attempted to work on this idea and offer different versions of a pretence account of irony.

Although it has been confronted by the echoic theory from the beginning, the pretence theory of irony is no doubt one of the main pragmatic approaches to this phenomenon.

4.6 SUGGESTED READING

4.6.1 Clark and Gerrig's Pretence Theory

The pretence theory was presented by Clark and Gerrig in the following paper:

Clark, H. H. & Richard J. Gerrig. 1984. On the pretense theory of irony. *Journal of Experimental Psychology: General* 113(1): 121–26.

4.6 Suggested Reading

4.6.2 Criticisms of the Pretence Theory

Sperber and Wilson have been the main critics of the pretence theory of irony. Their criticisms are summarized in the following works:

Sperber, D. 1984. Verbal irony: pretense or echoic mention? *Journal of Experimental Psychology: General* 113(1): 130–436.

Wilson, D. 2006. The pragmatics of verbal irony: echo or pretense? *Lingua* 116: 1722–43.

Wilson, D. & D. Sperber. 2012. *Meaning and Relevance*. Cambridge: Cambridge University Press.

4.6.3 Some Developments

These are the main works of the authors working on irony and pretence that I have mentioned earlier:

Currie, G. 2006. Why irony is pretense. In *The Architecture of the Imagination*, ed. S. Nichols, 111–33. Oxford: Oxford University Press.

Kumon-Nakamura, S., S. Glucksberg & M. Brown. 1995. How about another piece of pie: the allusional pretense theory of discourse irony. *Journal of Experimental Psychology: General* 124(1): 3–21.

Recanati, F. 2004. *Literal Meaning*. Cambridge: Cambridge University Press. 2007. Indexicality, context and pretense. In *Pragmatics*, ed. N. Burton-Roberts, 213–29. Basingstoke: Palgrave Macmillan.

Walton, K. 1990. *Mimesis as Make-Believe: On the Foundations of the Representational Arts*. Cambridge, MA: Harvard University Press. 2017. Meiosis, hyperbole, irony. *Philosophical Studies* 174(1): 105–20.

5 Attitude Expression in Irony

In the preceding three chapters, I introduced the main pragmatic theories of ironic communication. At this stage, it is evident that irony is conceived differently by the competing theories: according to Grice, it is a figurative case in which the literal meaning is made as if to say and the opposite implicated; for Sperber and Wilson, it is a case of echoic attribution; and for Clark and Gerrig, irony should be understood in terms of pretence. However, there is a point of departure that all these accounts share: in irony, the speaker does not *say* (or properly assert) the literal meaning of the utterance; she does something different. All authors appear to agree on this issue, and they all attempt to offer a suitable explanation for it – they all attempt to explain what it is that the ironic speaker does instead. The differences between the theories arise from the different explanations the authors offer for the same issue.

This is not the only point of agreement among the pragmatic theories of irony. When discussing a pragmatic conception of irony, it is unanimously accepted that attitude expression plays a key role in ironic communication. The importance of this element was signalled by Grice, as I mentioned in Section 2.1. Let us recall the example with which he illustrated this point.

> A and B are walking down the street, and they both see a car with a shattered window. B says:
>
> (4) Look, that car has all its windows intact.
>
> (Grice 1967b/89: 53)

According to Grice, utterance **(4)** apparently fulfils all conditions of ironic communication (the speaker puts forward a literal meaning that she blatantly does not believe to be true), but it is still not irony. Grice's explanation is straightforward: an element is missing in this example that prevents it from being a genuine instance of irony. What this

5 Attitude Expression in Irony

utterance lacks is the expression of a feeling, attitude or evaluation on the part of the speaker.

> [I]rony is intimately connected with the expression of a feeling, attitude, or evaluation. I cannot say something ironically unless what I say is intended to reflect a hostile or derogatory judgment or a feeling such as indignation or contempt. (Grice 1967b/89: 53-54)

This excerpt and the example of the shattered window gave rise to the second issue on which all theories converge: there is something about the expression of an attitude that appears essential in ironic communication. All accounts after Grice incorporate this element in their explanations. This initial agreement is short-lived, however – positions have diverged with regard to explaining the role this attitude plays in irony.

Most theories agree that attitude expression is crucial in irony, but they also claim that this attitude can be positive as well as negative. I will elaborate on this standard position next. However, I would like to focus on a different position as well – that which maintains that we always convey negative attitudes in irony. I will do so in Section 5.2.

Attitude

All theories agree that an attitude is expressed when being ironic. However, they do not call this attitude by the same name.

- *Grice* speaks of a feeling, attitude, evaluation, opinion or judgement:

  > [I]rony is intimately connected with the expression of a *feeling, attitude* or *evaluation*. I cannot say something ironically unless what I say is intended to reflect a hostile or derogatory *judgment* or a *feeling* such as indignation or contempt. (Grice 1967b/89: 54, my emphasis)

- *Sperber and Wilson* are more concise than Grice, speaking only of the attitude of the ironic speaker:

  > The *attitude* expressed by an ironical utterance is invariably of the rejecting or disapproving kind. The speaker dissociates herself from the opinion echoed and indicates that she does not hold it herself. (Sperber & Wilson 1986/95: 239, my emphasis)

- *Clark and Gerrig* adopt Grice's view: they repeat his words in addressing the attitude of the ironic speaker (Clark & Gerrig 1984: 122).

5 ATTITUDE EXPRESSION IN IRONY

- *Haverkate* mentions a qualifying judgement or qualification:

  > For present purposes, it is important to emphasize that whatever the type of assertive act may be, the intention of the ironic speaker is to express a *qualifying judgment*. It has often been pointed out that ironic *qualifications* are depreciatory, since they serve the particular purpose of criticizing the behavior of the interlocutor or other persons. (Haverkate 1990: 90, my emphasis)

- *I have claimed* that ironic speakers criticize, which means expressing a critical attitude:

  > In other words, in being ironic, the speaker expresses a critical *attitude* – a negatively evaluative *propositional attitude*. The speaker has a critical attitude – that very attitude she has expressed – if she is sincere when making that criticism. (Garmendia 2010: 403, my emphasis)

Thus, the point of agreement in these theories goes by the names of feeling, evaluation, attitude, qualification and judgement (and there may certainly be more). Here I will use the term 'attitude'.

Activity 5 Attitude Expression in Irony

We have already verified the speaker's attitude in your samples of irony in previous activities, but it is time to delve deeper. To start with, consider each of your ironic utterances and determine

1. Does the speaker express an attitude (qualification, judgement, feeling, evaluation)?
2. To whom/what is this attitude directed? (Who/what does it evaluate or judge?)

Discussion

(0)   That was a clumsy woman driving.

1. *Yes.* The speaker, Maia, expresses an attitude: her disapproving qualification, reproving judgement, feeling of rejection or negative evaluation.
2. The speaker's attitude is directed at the hearer, Ku – and more distantly, maybe, at the common sexist assumption that women cannot drive.

5.1 IRONY IS SOMETIMES POSITIVE: THE ASYMMETRY ISSUE

Irony always communicates an attitude, and this is something on which we may agree overall. However, Grice's words appear to indicate that he wished to make an additional claim regarding this point, namely, that it is not any type of attitude that we will find in irony but an attitude characterized by Grice as a hostile or derogatory judgement or a feeling such as indignation or contempt – an attitude of a negative nature, whichever way you frame it. He further claimed:

> I can for example say *What a scoundrel you are!* when I am well disposed toward you, but to say that will be playful, not ironical. (Grice 1967b/89: 54)

Thus, it appears that Grice did not merely claim that it is essential to express an attitude in irony; he also wanted to signal that this attitude is always of the negative type – although he did not use the term 'negative' and did not say more on the issue. However, that is a condition that the rest of the theories are not prepared to accept.

The possibility of being ironic without expressing a negative attitude has been considered plausible by most theories, including Sperber and Wilson's echoic theory, Clark and Gerrig's pretence theory, Kreuz and Glucksberg's echoic reminder theory, Kumon-Nakamura et al.'s allusional pretence theory and Haverkate's speech act approach to irony. This is due to the existence of certain cases that are apparently ironic and not negative and that would demonstrate the possibility of being ironic while expressing something positive, such as the following:

> Nancy and her friend Jane were planning a trip to the beach. 'It's probably going to rain tomorrow', said Jane, who was always trying, with little success, to predict the weather. The next day was a warm and sunny one. As she looked out the window, Nancy said:
>
> (37) This certainly is awful weather.
>
> (Kreuz & Glucksberg 1989: 377)

> Suppose that I have a friend who is not very self-confident and after an examination he says: 'I'm going to fail this exam. I did it all wrong'. After some days, I meet him and he tells me that he has passed the exam with a very good mark. Then, I could ironically say:

(38) Oh yes, you have failed, you did it all wrong, you are a very bad student!

(Alba-Juez 1995: 11)

Spoken by your stockbroker on calling for the third time to announce unexpected dividends:

(39) Sorry to keep bothering you like this.

(Brown 1980: 114, quoted in Attardo 2000: 796)

An adult addressing a child:

(40) Oh, how small you have grown!

(Haverkate 1990: 90)

In a conversation between two lovers:

(41) I don't like you at all!

(Haverkate 1990: 90)

As the majority of theories of irony accept that such cases are ironic and express a positive attitude, they consequently admit that positive irony does exist. Thus, we shall always find an attitude expressed in irony, but this attitude will not always be of the negative type.

However, all these theories also accept that these cases of irony without criticism are not as common as negative irony. Thus, it is concluded that the attitude conveyed via irony is *typically* (even if not always) negative. This imbalance creates what is called the 'asymmetry issue' of irony: positive ironic examples are much scarcer than negative ones.

Negative

I will use the term 'negative', but this idea has also been referred to differently by the different theories.

- *Grice* compares the attitude in irony with hostility, derogatoriness, indignation or contempt:

  > I cannot say something ironically unless what I say is intended to reflect a *hostile* or *derogatory* judgment or a feeling such as *indignation* or *contempt*. (Grice 1967b/89: 54, my emphasis)

- *Sperber and Wilson* state that ironic speakers convey a dissociative attitude, but they acknowledge this type to be quite broad:

5.1 Irony Is Sometimes Positive: The Asymmetry Issue 93

> Dissociative attitudes themselves vary quite widely, falling anywhere on a spectrum from *amused tolerance* through various shades of *resignation* or *disappointment* to *contempt, disgust, outrage* or *scorn*. The attitudes prototypical of verbal irony are generally seen as coming from the milder, or more controlled, part of the range. (Wilson & Sperber 2012: 130, my emphasis)

- *Haverkate* mentions depreciatory qualifications:

> It has often been pointed out that ironic qualifications are *depreciatory*, since they serve the particular purpose of criticizing the behavior of the interlocutor or other persons. (Haverkate 1990: 90, my emphasis)

- I call the attitude of ironic speakers critical, and I define this criticism as a negative evaluation:

> In other words, in being ironic, the speaker expresses a *critical* attitude – a *negatively* evaluative propositional attitude. (Garmendia 2010: 403, my emphasis)

Thus, the ensuing question would be: why does this asymmetry issue exist? That is, why is irony typically negative and only sometimes positive? Different theories provide different answers to this question. Let me briefly recall them in order to view the differences and the points of agreement.

- For Sperber and Wilson, irony always contains an echo. A speaker can echo many different types of sources, particular or general, explicit or implicit. Herein lies the key of the asymmetry issue: positive irony typically requires a source for the echo, an explicit prior doubt to have been expressed or entertained, whereas negative irony does not. That is what makes positive irony more difficult and thus scarcer.

  In addition, why is it that positive irony requires prior doubt, while negative irony does not? Culturally defined rules are the answer.

> Standards or rules of behavior are culturally defined, commonly known, and frequently invoked; they are thus always available for echoic mention. On the other hand, critical judgments are particular to a given individual or occasion, and are thus only occasionally available for echoic mention. Hence, it is always possible to say ironically of a failure *That was a great success*, since it is normal to hope for the success of a given course of action. However, to say of a success *That was a failure* without the irony falling flat, the speaker must be able to refer back to prior

doubts or fears, which he can then echo ironically. (Sperber & Wilson 1981: 312)

- Kreuz and Glucksberg's echoic reminder theory is similar to Sperber and Wilson's, and it is therefore the explanation they offer for the asymmetry issue. According to this account, irony consists of an echoic reminder, and this reminder can be either implicit or explicit. Positive irony, again, would require an explicit antecedent of which to be reminded, in contrast to negative irony, because we do share positive norms of which to be reminded but not negative ones. Hence, the reason for the asymmetry.

> Implicit reminding, therefore, is sufficient for positive statements intended ironically because there are positive norms to be reminded of. In contrast, implicit reminding should not be sufficient for negative statements intended ironically because normally there are no implicit negative norms to be reminded of. (Kreuz & Glucksberg 1989: 376)

- Clark and Gerrig claim that when being ironic, a speaker pretends to be someone else. However, people typically view the world positively, particularly those whom they called the 'people in ignorance', those who ironic speakers typically pretend to be. This is why in irony we typically pretend something positive to obtain a negative result.

> An ironist is more likely to say 'What a clever idea' of a bad idea than 'What a stupid idea' of a good one. Why? As Jorgensen et al. point out, people tend to see the world according to norms of success and excellence, as Pollyannas who view the world through rose-colored glasses (Boucher & Osgood 1969). People in ignorance should cling especially tightly to these norms. In the pretense theory, this is just the sort of person ironists pretend to be. (Clark & Gerrig 1984: 122)

- Kumon-Nakamura and colleagues' allusional pretence theory of irony claims that every irony makes allusion to a prior prediction, expectation, preference or norm that has been violated. As positive expectations are relatively more frequent than negative expectations, ironic speakers can more easily allude to them, which is why negative irony is more frequent.

> Ironic expressions can generally allude to implicit social norms and expectations. Therefore, when negative expectations are available, negative statements regarding positive situations can be used ironically. Positive statements regarding negative situations can be used ironically whether or not there exists a specific negative expectation, because positive statements can

5.2 Irony Is Always Negative

always allude to general positive expectations or norms. (Kumon-Nakamura et al. 1995: 13)

The explanations of the asymmetry issue follow, as we can observe, a similar pattern. The theories explain the asymmetry in irony based on their conceptions of irony; that is, if they claim that irony consists in echoing, reminding, pretending or alluding, they explain that positive rules, standards, norms or expectations are more common and thus easier to echo, remind, pretend or allude to. Aside from the terminological issue, all these theories appear to agree on where the foundations of the asymmetry issue lay.

Activity 5.1 Positive Irony

In Activity 5, you noted the attitudes that your speakers convey. Consider these attitudes again.

1. Are they positive or negative types of attitudes? (Reproving, mocking, teasing, blaming, critical or approving, praising, complimenting?)

Discussion

(0)   That was a clumsy woman driving.

1. The speaker's attitude is reproving and mocking – negative.

If in all your samples the speaker expresses a negative type of attitude, put them on hold for the rest of this chapter, and we will return to them later. Now please think about a possible candidate for positive irony: an ironic utterance that apparently blames but actually praises. You will use this new example as a sample for the next activities in this chapter.

In respect to my sample, I will use the positive-looking variant I introduced in Activity 3.1B.

5.2 IRONY IS ALWAYS NEGATIVE

All pragmatic accounts of irony attempt to explain the asymmetry issue, yet there is a prior crucial point that deserves our attention: does this asymmetry actually exist in irony? I am not questioning whether positive irony is less frequent than negative irony – as

96   5 ATTITUDE EXPRESSION IN IRONY

I just stated, all the theories appear to agree that irony is at least *typically* negative. What I am questioning is whether there really are instances of positive irony that would create an imbalance.

The main reason why most pragmatic theories claim that irony is *typically but not always* negative is the assumption that there are certain cases that are ironic even if the speaker expresses a positive attitude. These cases are scarcer than traditional negative irony, but they exist – or so they claim. A detailed analysis of the allegedly positive instances of irony is in order, and I will proceed with such in the following two subsections.

5.2.1 False Positives

Among examples **(37)–(41)** that I have presented as candidates for positive irony, there are several differences. The first two cases illustrate examples of irony that follow the same pattern as typically known cases of negative irony, with the only apparent difference being that now the speaker appears to blame while actually intending to praise. This similarity is most obvious in example **(37)**, which is evidently the reverse case of Sperber and Wilson's picnic example:

> Nancy and her friend Jane were planning a trip to the beach. 'It's probably going to rain tomorrow' said Jane, who was always trying, with little success, to predict the weather. The next day was a warm and sunny one. As she looked out the window, Nancy said:
>
> (37) This certainly is awful weather.
>
>   (Kreuz & Glucksberg 1989: 377)
>
> PETER: It's a lovely day for a picnic.
>
> They go for a picnic and it rains.
>
> MARY (sarcastically):
>
> (15) It's a lovely day for a picnic, indeed.
>
>   (Sperber & Wilson 1986/95: 239)

The second scene exemplifies a traditional instance of negative irony: Mary apparently says that it is beautiful weather, but she actually communicates through irony that it is cold and stormy, awful weather for a picnic. In contrast, the first scene would be an example of so-called positive irony: Nancy apparently complains or regrets that the weather is awful while she ironically communicates that the weather is warm and

5.2 Irony Is Always Negative

sunny and is ideal for a trip to the beach. Thus, allegedly, in the first case Mary blames by praising, and in the second case Nancy praises by blaming, and that would be the only difference between these two instances of irony: the first one is positive irony, and the second one is negative irony.

Many of the cases accepted as positive irony are of this type. It appears to me, however, that they are admitted as positive irony too easily. A further analysis will show the issue under a different light. Moreover, it will be crucial to bear in mind something that I noted when addressing the shortcomings of the Gricean approach: ironic utterances typically communicate a first implicature that appears closely related to the literal meaning of the utterance – the implicature I call the 'bridge content' of the utterance. This implicature, however, is no more than one among other implicatures with which it completes what the speaker intends to communicate with her ironic utterance.

Irony is a complex phenomenon, and it is typically grounded in rich contextual information. If we consider the picnic example and recall that this morning Peter said that it was a lovely day for a picnic, we will understand that Mary, when uttering **(15)** 'It's a lovely day for a picnic, indeed' has communicated that it is an awful day for a picnic as well as something else: that Peter erroneously predicted the weather, and it is because of his mistake that they are currently standing in the rain. The implicature that it is an awful day for a picnic (or maybe, more precisely, that it is not a lovely day for a picnic) is just one of the implicatures communicated by the speaker – it is the bridge content that will help the hearer infer the remainder of the implicatures that have been communicated as well.

It is not always easy to define and specify what it is exactly that a speaker intended to communicate via irony, but an effort should be made to be fair with the speaker's intentions and describe the ironic meaning accordingly. If we do so with the examples that are apparently positive irony, things may present differently from what they appeared. This is the case of the beach example: Nancy uttered **(37)** 'This certainly is awful weather' when the sun was shining, and she may have intended to communicate via irony that it was a beautiful day. However, we also know that on the previous day Jane had predicted that it would rain.[1] Thus, Nancy is now attempting to communicate something else as well: that Jane wrongly predicted the weather (and that they almost did not go

---

[1] In fact, Wilson and Sperber (2012: 127) note that it is Jane's wrong prediction that allows Nancy to be ironic when uttering **(37)** 'This is certainly awful weather'. Alternatively, if Jane's prediction did not exist, Nancy's utterance would not count as ironic when uttered on such a beautiful day. The authors conclude

98   5 ATTITUDE EXPRESSION IN IRONY

to the beach because of that, that Jane is a terrible forecaster, etc.). All these further implicatures complete, along with the bridge implicature of the utterance, the ironic content that the speaker intended to communicate. Furthermore, if we consider what the speaker has communicated overall, we will notice that the point of Nancy's utterance is to blame Jane and not to praise the good weather. Even in the apparently most positive scenario, even when the sun is shining and we are about to enjoy a beautiful day at the beach, we are able to make an utterance that expresses a negative attitude.

The second example of positive irony shows a similar pattern.

> Suppose that I have a friend who is not very self-confident, and after an examination he says: 'I'm going to fail this exam. I did it all wrong'. After some days, I meet him and he tells me that he has passed the exam with a very good mark. Then, I could ironically say:
>
> (38) Oh yes, you have failed, you did it all wrong, you are a very bad student!
>
> (Alba-Juez 1995: 11)

According to the standard explanation, the literal meaning of my utterance is negative, but if we consider the context, we may understand that I am being ironic: I have communicated something positive by being ironic. Thus, I intend to praise my friend with my apparent criticism. While in the case of negative irony we criticize by praising, in the case of positive irony we praise by criticizing.

Thus far, it appears that this example is one of so-called positive irony because criticism is lacking. However, again, bearing in mind the context of the utterance, what did I intend to communicate by uttering **(38)**? I may have communicated that my friend performed brilliantly on his exam and that he is a very good student, but there is something else about my utterance – that was just the implicature that will work as a bridge to arrive at further ironic implicatures. Otherwise, the utterance would be uninformative. The information that my friend performed brilliantly on his exam is trivial. In fact, for the audience to understand that I am being ironic, they must know beforehand that my friend actually did a very good job on the exam. If this positive meaning had exhausted what I communicated with

---

from this evidence that positive irony requires an explicit antecedent – their argument to explain the asymmetry issue. However, a more immediate conclusion appears to be that only when a negative attitude is included does the irony arise in this case.

5.2 Irony Is Always Negative

(38), it would be no more than a reminder of what everyone who understands it already knows.[2]

However, knowing the context as we do, we can correctly guess that there is indeed something else that I intended to convey with **(38)**: that I am bored with my friend's complaining, that I will not believe him anymore, that he was being foolish and so on. All these negative evaluations were communicated by my uttering **(38)** ironically.

Thus, in these first two examples of alleged positive irony, the speakers have communicated a negative attitude – even if it is a - beautiful day and even if my friend performed brilliantly on his exam. Should we accept, then, that they are truly cases of positive irony? It does not appear so. Even if we accepted that the speakers communicated, via irony, that the weather is beautiful and that my friend did well on the exam, this would not prevent the examples from being negative irony, as the speakers also communicated something negative, a criticism towards Jane and towards my friend.

It would be useful to notice that even in the typical examples unanimously accepted as negative, the speaker can communicate something positive – apart from a negative attitude, of course. Let me revisit example **(5)**:

> During the precept, Danny was dominating the discussion. He certainly seemed to be familiar with the subject, but he was obnoxious in the way he showed off his knowledge. Jesse, one of Danny's classmates, said:
>
> (5) You sure know a lot.
>
> (Kumon-Namakura et al. 1995: 7)

Here Jesse has communicated that Danny behaved pretentiously, and that is all we required to consider this a negative irony. Nevertheless, if we attempt to detail the speaker's ironic meaning in this case, we can also find positive elements there – that Danny knows a lot, for instance. However, this would not suffice to call into question the negative nature of Jesse's utterance – he was criticizing Danny, and that is sufficient.

A similar argument will apply to this first type of positive irony: it may convey something positive, but that is not sufficient to consider it an instance of positive irony. To argue that it is not an instance of typical, common, negative irony, we must demonstrate that it does not express a negative attitude. However, it fails this condition, and

---

[2] Garmendia & Korta (2007) develop this idea.

100   5 ATTITUDE EXPRESSION IN IRONY

Activity 5.2.1 False Positives

Let us consider the example of positive irony you selected in Activity 5.1.

1. Would you say that the speaker also conveyed something negative with her irony?

If so, your sample is what I have called a 'false positive'. For the next activity, try to think of an example of irony that expresses a positive attitude and no negative attitude.

2. Do you think instead that there is no negative attitude in the example you chose? Then keep your example for the next activity.

Discussion

Ku (who always claims that women are terrible drivers) witnesses a woman elegantly manoeuvring a car into a small and awkward parking spot. Ku himself then exclaims,

(0')   That was a clumsy woman driving.

1. In this variant of the example, the speaker is Ku, and he is apparently blaming the female driver but actually praising her for driving skills – this is why this variant appeared to be a candidate for positive irony. However, there is something else that Ku has arguably expressed with his ironic utterance – that he was wrong when he claimed that women are reckless drivers. This latter evaluation is clearly negative, and it is directed at Ku himself. My candidate for positive irony thus turns out to be a false positive.

---

thus there is no reason to assume that it is special,[3] that it is not an instance of typical, common, negative irony.

5.2.2 Controversial Cases

In the preceding subsection, I considered a type of irony that has typically been understood as a positive form of irony. It is a type of irony that includes a positive attitude, and this is why it has been

---

[3] Unless we want to claim that the peculiarity of these cases is nothing more than having a positive-looking bridge content. However, the particularities of positive irony have traditionally been understood as stronger than this. In fact, if this were the only peculiarity of positive irony, ironic utterances such as **(5)** should also count as positive (as **(5)** has a positively evaluative bridge content).

5.2 Irony Is Always Negative 101

classified as positive. However, if we pay closer attention to the context and specify what it is that the speakers are communicating ironically, we realize that a negative attitude is also conveyed in these examples. This is why they are questionable candidates for positive irony.

However, there are other types of alleged positive irony as well. In particular, there are certain cases that are considered to be ironic, that express a positive attitude and that apparently do not include a negative element in what is communicated. Examples **(39)–(41)** are of this type.

> Spoken by your stockbroker on calling for the third time to announce unexpected dividends:
>
> (39) Sorry to keep bothering you like this.
>
> > (Brown 1980: 114, quoted in Attardo 2000: 796)
>
> An adult addressing a child:
>
> (40) Oh, how small you have grown!
>
> > (Haverkate 1990: 90)
>
> In a conversation between two lovers:
>
> (41) I don't like you at all!
>
> > (Haverkate 1990: 90)

These three utterances are proposed as cases of positive irony. They fulfil the two conditions that the preceding two candidates also satisfied; that is, they are instances of irony, and they show an apparent negative evaluation in order to communicate something positive: with **(39)**, my stockbroker apparently expresses his apologies, but he actually wants to convey his enthusiasm; when uttering **(40)**, an adult is apparently saying that the child has not grown since the last time, but she is really communicating that the child has grown a lot; when a lover utters **(41)**, she is apparently claiming that she does not like the hearer but in fact is communicating that she likes her a lot. Thus, they are cases of irony, and they convey something positive.

There is also a third condition that these three examples appear to fulfil, which the previous two examples did not. From the (succinct) contextual information we have available, it appears that no negative attitude is expressed along with the positive attitude they convey. There is nothing negative in what the stockbroker, the adult and the lover intended to communicate when uttering **(39)–(41)** ironically.

102   5 ATTITUDE EXPRESSION IN IRONY

In a nutshell, these instances appear to be ironic, positive and non-negative. There are two possible positions at this stage.

The general position is to admit these as cases of positive irony and, therefore, to admit that irony is not necessarily negative. As it is agreed that most irony continues to be negative, the asymmetry issue is undeniable and must be explained. This is the line of thinking that most theories follow, including Sperber and Wilson, Clark and Gerrig, Kreuz and Glucksberg, Haverkate, and the majority of authors I have considered thus far.

In contrast, I still claim that irony is always and essentially negative. I believe Grice gave us a hint on this issue, which has often gone unnoticed. He stated that we can certainly call someone towards whom we are well disposed a scoundrel, but he explains that to say so would not be ironic but *playful* (Grice 1967b/89: 54). I basically agree with Grice on this issue. We can certainly say to our lover that we don't love her or to a child that she has not grown. However, we are not being ironic when we say these sorts of things.

In previous work (Garmendia, 2010), I have claimed that these latter examples are not ironic if they do not hide some type of criticism in the absent context. If all that the adult is communicating when uttering **(40)** 'Oh, how small you have grown!' is that the child has grown a lot, then that is not irony. The same applies to the other two examples: if they are intending to be ironic, then the stockbroker must have intended to communicate something more than his enthusiasm and the lover something more than her evident love. Otherwise, these would be nonsensical cases of irony. What we grasp in these examples is just a trivial implicature, the strongly communicated bridge content of the utterance. This utterance typically leads us to further ironic implicatures – it is uninformative and even trivial on its own. Thus, if that were all that the speaker intended to communicate in these cases, these utterances would appear uninformative and pointless. We can compare these cases with Grice's original example of the shattered window, in which a speaker unsuccessfully tries to be ironic by merely saying the opposite of what she believes (Garmendia 2010: 409).

Moreover, if we change the context to include a negative attitude in what is communicated, then these cases are no longer controversial, as they become unquestionably ironic. Let us consider the following variant of example **(39)**:

5.2 *Irony Is Always Negative* 103

Claudio's stockbroker calls for the third time to announce unexpected dividends. Claudio answers rudely: 'You again? What is it now?' The broker replies,

(42) Sorry to keep bothering you like this.

(Garmendia 2010: 411)

This is, I would venture, a clearer ironic utterance, but it is clearly negative as well: Claudio is obviously criticizing the broker's insistent calls. It is because we can now grasp further ironic implicatures and a negative attitude is present that the irony becomes more blatant. This would show, again, that irony is essentially negative and that there is no irony that does not express, in one way or another, a negative attitude.

> I have shown that if what is communicated is critical, then the examples are ironic, whereas if we do not know what is being communicated, they are nonsense, given that it would be nonsensical to say (or make as if to say) something while communicating its opposite, when that opposite is evident both to the speaker and to the hearer. (Garmendia 2010: 411)

This defence of the negative nature of irony has encountered a certain amount of support (Dynel 2013a, 2013b; Garmendia 2010, 2011, 2015; Hirsch 2010). Nevertheless, the dominant position is the one that accepts some cases of positive irony and consequently discards the essential condition of the negative attitude in irony.

Activity 5.2.2 Controversial Cases

Please consider the example of irony that made it through the last activity – an ironic utterance through which the speaker expresses something positive and nothing negative.

1. Do you still consider that it does not include any type of negative expression (you may have to develop the context in certain cases)?
2. Do you still believe that it is a case of irony?

If you answered both questions affirmatively, then you agree with the existence of positive irony.

104   5 ATTITUDE EXPRESSION IN IRONY

5.3 THE TINGE HYPOTHESIS

Thus far, the role played in irony by the expression of a negative attitude appears to be a complicated matter. Since Grice, every theory accepts that attitude expression is crucial in irony, but in light of a number of positive-looking examples, most of them also assume that this attitude can sometimes be positive. A few authors still maintain that positive irony is not truly positive or truly ironic, remaining faithful to Grice's belief in the negative nature of irony.

At this point, it is worth paying attention to the 'tinge hypothesis' (Dews & Winner 1995, 1999; Dews et al. 1995). It is not exactly a theory arguing against or in favour of the possibility of being both positive and ironic – in fact, it assumes the existence of positive irony – but it makes interesting claims related to the evaluative tone of ironic utterances and could be useful to shed light on this debate.

These authors' challenge consists in explaining why we use irony. Indeed, there must exist benefits to being ironic because the risks generated by irony must be compensated somehow. Otherwise, there would be no strong incentive to be ironic. As the authors state, quoting Roberts and Kreuz: 'The benefits of using figurative language must outweigh the potential costs of being misunderstood' (Roberts & Kreuz 1994: 159).

It is in aiming to explain the social functions of irony that these authors postulate the tinge hypothesis. According to this hypothesis, ironic utterances are based on an opposition between meanings – the literal meaning of the utterance and the intended meaning communicated ironically – and the evaluative tone of the literal meaning tinges the hearer's perception of the speaker's intended meaning. When a speaker uses a positive literal meaning to communicate a negative ironic meaning (as in typical irony), this ironic meaning is coloured by the positivity of the literal meaning. In contrast, when a speaker uses a negative literal meaning to communicate a positive ironic meaning (as in positive irony), the negativity of the literal meaning colours the ironic meaning. Essentially, what these authors are suggesting is that certain aspects of the literal meaning are processed when interpreting an ironic utterance and that these aspects tinge or colour the hearer's interpretation of the ironic meaning. They present several experiments that would support this hypothesis.

This colouring would have an immediate consequence: hearers would interpret ironic criticisms as less negative than their literal counterparts and ironic compliments as less praising than their literal

5.4 Suggested Reading

counterparts. This would explain why we choose to be ironic, even if it involves the risk of being misunderstood (I focus on the risks of being ironic in Chapter 6). As the non-intended literal meaning somewhat shades what is communicated ironically, irony can be used to express 'subtle shadings of meanings about attitudes and beliefs' (Dews & Winner 1995: 15).

The motivation for being ironically critical follows easily from there: a speaker will use irony when she intends to express a negative evaluation yet wants to mitigate the hearer's reaction. In this line, Dews and colleagues also claim that ironic criticism damages the relationship between speaker and hearer less than literal criticism (Dews et al. 1995).[4]

Furthermore, ironic compliments are used when the speaker wants to express a tinge of criticism along with the positive compliment:

> By complimenting ironically, the speaker may want to appear to compliment while actually criticizing. The target may have done nothing wrong, but may have inspired envy or annoyance on the part of the speaker. (Dews & Winner 1995: 16)

It thus follows from this account that positive irony does exist, but it is coloured with a negative tinge. This may be viewed as an intermediate position in the debate regarding positive irony: these authors assert that there are cases in which a speaker is ironic and positive; however, the positive meaning conveyed has been muted by the literal meaning and shows a negative tinge.

5.4 SUGGESTED READING

5.4.1 The Attitude in Irony

Sperber and Wilson have devoted many pages to the analysis of attitude communication in irony. In their first paper on the subject (Sperber & Wilson 1981), they had already outlined their view of the issue. In Wilson & Sperber (1992), they delve into this question and elaborate on Grice's non-ironic example of the shattered window. In their most recent paper on irony (Wilson & Sperber 2012), they summarize their view regarding the attitude expression concerning irony and the asymmetry issue resulting from it. They also touch on how pretence and Gricean theories could explain this matter.

---

[4] This is in line with the claims in Brown & Levinson's (1987) politeness theory.

106   5 ATTITUDE EXPRESSION IN IRONY

Sperber, D. & D. Wilson. 1981. Irony and the use-mention distinction. In *Radical Pragmatics*, ed. P. Cole, 295–318. New York: Academic Press.

Wilson, D. & D. Sperber. 1992. On verbal irony. *Lingua* 87: 53–76.

Wilson, D. & D. Sperber. 2012. *Meaning and Relevance*. Cambridge: Cambridge University Press.

In the following papers, Kumon-Nakamura and colleagues present results from an experiment testing the relation between positive/negative irony and the allusion to a precedent proposition. Similarly, Alan Partington presents a corpus-based analysis focused on the reversal of evaluation in irony, and Laura Alba-Juez and Salvatore Attardo present the results of a study on the evaluative character of verbal irony.

Alba-Juez, L. & S. Attardo. 2014. The evaluative palette of verbal irony. In *Evaluation in Context*, ed. G. Thompson & L. Alba-Juez, 93–115. Amsterdam: John Benjamins.

Kumon-Nakamura, S., S. Glucksberg & M. Brown. 1995. How about another piece of pie: the allusional pretense theory of discourse irony. *Journal of Experimental Psychology: General* 124(1): 3–21.

Partington, A. 2007. Irony and reversal of evaluation. *Journal of Pragmatics* 39: 1547–69.

5.4.2 Irony Is Negative

These papers by Dynel and Garmendia advocate for an essentially negative view of irony.

Dynel, M. 2013a. Irony from a neo-Gricean perspective: on untruthfulness and evaluative implicature. *Intercultural Pragmatics* 10(3): 403–31.

Garmendia, J. 2010. Irony is critical. *Pragmatics and Cognition* 18(2): 397–421. 2015. A (neo-)Gricean account of irony: an answer to relevance theory. *International Review of Pragmatics* 7: 40–79.

5.4.3 The Tinge Hypothesis

The basics of this hypothesis are compiled in the following papers:

Dews, S. & E. Winner. 1995. Muting the meaning: a social function of irony. *Metaphor and Symbolic Activity* 10: 3–19.

Dews, S. & E. Winner. 1999. Obligatory processing of literal and nonliteral meanings in verbal irony. *Journal of Pragmatics* 31: 1579–99.

Dews, S., J. Kaplan & E. Winner. 1995. Why not say it directly? The social functions of irony. *Discourse Processes* 19: 347–67.

6 Clues of Irony

Whenever someone speaks ironically, she puts forward a meaning that she does not intend to communicate – something that every pragmatic theory is prepared to accept. A major risk is associated with being ironic: a hearer who does not recognize the speaker's irony will believe that the speaker has committed herself to that literal meaning; that is, he will assume that she intended to communicate that literal meaning. Moreover, a speaker speaking ironically always has the intention of expressing an attitude that is typically negative. Thus, misunderstandings in irony result in misunderstandings involving the speaker's attitudes and criticisms. I will elaborate on the risks of being ironic in Section 6.1.

To avoid misunderstandings, ironic speakers can resort to using clues. Much has been written regarding ironic speakers' clues. Several have garnered considerable attention from authors working on pragmatics, including the speaker's tone of voice and stylistic choices. I will introduce these traditional clues of irony in Section 6.2. Then, in Section 6.3, I will explain why I consider that several other features of irony should be included in this list as well. This view of the issue will evolve into a proposal for an inclusive theory of ironic communication, which I will present in Section 6.4.

6.1 THE RISKS OF IRONY

In Chapter 1, I mentioned the case of a cover from the magazine *The New Yorker*. This cover was published in the summer of 2008, when the United States was absorbed by the presidential election campaign. Much had been said about candidate Barack Obama during the previous months, or rather *against* him, including that he was a radical Muslim conspiring against the United States, anti-patriotic

108 6 CLUES OF IRONY

and a friend of terrorists and that his wife, Michelle Obama, was potentially a successor to the Black Panthers.

It was in this general context that the cover by Barry Blitt was published, on 21 July 2008.[1] Its title was 'The Politics of Fear', and it showed a scene in the Oval Office starring Barack and Michelle Obama. On one side, Michelle Obama appears with an Afro hairstyle, dressed in military attire and carrying an AK-47. On the other side, bumping fists with his wife, we see Barack Obama in Muslim clothing and wearing a turban. In the background, we can observe a portrait of Osama bin Laden hanging above a fireplace in which an American flag is burning.

Reactions were immediate. Obama's spokespeople branded the cover tasteless and offensive, and readers even threatened to cancel their subscriptions because they deemed the cover disgusting, gross or sick. It was interpreted as a highly offensive attack against the Obamas.

The magazine responded promptly. David Remnick, editor of *The New Yorker*, explained in an interview[2] that the cover was political satire and should not be interpreted literally. The intention was to 'hold up a mirror' to all the nonsense that had been published regarding Barack and Michelle Obama, their lack of patriotism and their radical ideologies. He admitted to being aware that the cover could be misinterpreted, but he claimed that the image was intended to be as clear as possible. Moreover, being familiar with *The New Yorker*'s stance (or, as he puts it, 'what we do and who we are') and knowing that political satire appears frequently in the magazine should have been sufficient for readers to see that the cover was not saying those things literally.

The cover is labelled satirical by the editor of the magazine, but what happened illustrates convincingly the risks implied in critical indirect forms of communication, particularly irony. Remnick's response provides a strong hint. The publishers were aware that the cover could be misinterpreted, as this risk is inherent in every ironic-sarcastic-satiric case. However, the editor believes that the cover had the elements to favour its correct understanding: readers are familiar with the magazine – and contextual information is vital in these cases. Moreover, the cover was thought to be sufficiently clear – hints and

---

[1] The cover can be found at www.newyorker.com/magazine/2008/07/21 (accessed April 2017).

[2] Which you can read at www.huffingtonpost.com/2008/07/13/david-remnick-on -emnew-yo_n_112456.html (accessed April 2017).

6.1 The Risks of Irony

clues are always useful when being indirectly critical. Remnick even explains that the cover was holding a mirror to widespread nonsense – and that is a close image to that of echoing.

This particular incident illustrates the issue I will address in the following sections. Ironic utterances, as cases of indirectly communicated criticisms, run the risk of confusing the hearer. Speakers typically use irony when they believe the hearer will be able to detect it. Hearers can do this (that is, they can recognize that the speaker is speaking ironically) by relying on contextual information, background or shared knowledge and familiarity with the speaker's beliefs and her way of expressing herself.

When a speaker and a hearer know each other well, the hearer can easily recognize that it is impossible for the speaker to have literally said *that* which she appears to be putting forward. Being familiar with each other's beliefs facilitates ironic communication between a speaker and a hearer. For instance, let us say that we observe someone attempting to park a car clumsily, and when the driver leaves the car, we note it is a woman, and I claim, 'Of course, it had to be a woman'. However, you know my feminist convictions, and you are confident that I do not believe that someone's gender can influence her ability to drive in any way. This background information, namely, this knowledge we share, is probably sufficient for you to understand that I cannot be saying those words *seriously*. You will require few clues to recognize that I am being ironic and communicating something different, maybe mocking people we both know, who could genuinely think that being a woman was the reason why the driver had such trouble parking.

Background knowledge is crucial in irony. In fact, people who know each other well typically require few clues when being ironic.

There is another level of familiarity that it is very important in irony as well. Certain speakers tend to frequently speak ironically.[3] This is another factor that can help the hearer to detect the irony, as he may expect the speaker to speak ironically – in other words, the hearer will be more vigilant with this type of speaker. Similarly, certain communication channels are also more prone to using irony than others: one expects a late night TV show host to use irony in her speeches or political commentaries but does not expect irony to appear in a piece of news in a newspaper.

---

[3] People who we typically would call 'ironic' – and notice that we would not do the same with speakers who frequently use metaphors; it would be strange to call them 'metaphoric' people.

110   6 CLUES OF IRONY

A final aspect is worth noting here. Contextual information also helps the hearer to identify the irony. It is always important to know when, where and in which situation the speaker said what she said in order to recognize her ironic intent. One's ironic remark regarding the weather can easily be recognized as ironic merely because it is raining or windy or whatever other fact that belongs to the meteorological context of the utterance.

We may find certain instances of irony in which background information relative to the speaker or hearer is crucial for the hearer's understanding of the irony. This is what occurs in Grice's example of the fine friend, where it is because the hearer knows what the speaker really believes regarding X that he can recognize the irony in utterance **(3)**:

> X, with whom A has been on close terms until now, has betrayed a secret of A's to a business rival. A and his audience both know this. A says:

> (3) X is a fine friend.

> (Grice 1967a/89: 34)

There are also cases in which it is the immediate context that helps the hearer in his detection of the irony. For example, it is, among other things, because it is raining at the time of the utterance that Peter recognizes Mary's ironic intent in **(15)**:

> PETER: It's a lovely day for a picnic.

> They go for a picnic and it rains.

> MARY (sarcastically):

> (15) It's a lovely day for a picnic, indeed.

> (Sperber & Wilson 1986/95: 239)

Thus, hearers use contextual and background information to interpret an ironic utterance correctly – just as they do with non-ironic utterances, obviously. However, sometimes a speaker decides that this may not be sufficient and uses additional elements to support the hearer in his endeavour. The goal is always to help the hearer recognize the irony and understand what the speaker intends to communicate. Some of these 'elements' – which are typically called 'clues' or 'cues' of irony – have drawn experts' attention for a long time. I will focus on them in Section 6.2.

6.1 The Risks of Irony

Activity 6.1 The Risks of Irony: Context and Background Information

Please return to the irony samples that you used in the first part of this book. Let us examine how speaker and hearer confront the risks of irony.

1. How does contextual or background information help the hearer in each case?

Discussion

In the ironic utterance I have been testing throughout these activities as my own sample, both elements are crucial for understanding the irony. When Maia uttered

(0)   That was a clumsy woman driving

the contextual information that the driver was not actually a woman and the shared background knowledge that Ku believes that women drive terribly were equally important for the hearer.

Benefits of Irony
(Or Why Are We Ironic, Even If It Is Risky?)

Irony has social benefits that compensate for the costs of the risks it entails.

- **Irony makes criticism gentler.** A negative attitude communicated ironically is not felt as threateningly as a negative attitude communicated directly, as some experiments have shown.[4]
- **Irony allows the hearer to save face.**[5] As it is an indirect form of expressing an attitude, irony allows the hearer to potentially escape from the negative attitude directed toward him: in those cases in which the hearer does not want to acknowledge the receipt of a negative attitude, he can opt to ignore the ironic

---

[4] It should be noted that certain authors have defended precisely the opposite claim: that criticism is enhanced when communicated through irony. Experimental studies show a mixed picture regarding this point. While some studies affirm that irony minimizes the negative impact of criticism (Dews & Winner 1995, 1999; Dews et al. 1995; Brown & Levinson 1987; Jorgensen 1996), others state precisely the opposite – that irony enhances such impact (Toplak & Katz 2000; Colston 1997; Colston & O'Brien 2000). See Filik et al. (2017) for a different position on this issue.

[5] I am using the notion of face as elaborated in Brown & Levinson's (1987) politeness theory.

content of the utterance and reply instead to the literal (and typically positive) meaning.

- **Irony allows the speaker to save face.** Irony enables the speaker to deny the responsibilities of having been ironically critical by allowing her to take a step back and defend a non-ironic interpretation of her utterance.

To speak ironically provides the speaker with the opportunity to sound gentler, to step back, if necessary, and to offer the hearer the option of ignoring the irony. Regarding the latter two, we could also rephrase them by saying that it is easier to lie regarding one's real intentions or to pretend to ignore others' real intentions when these have been expressed ironically and not directly.

6.2 TRADITIONAL CLUES

The ironic speaker, as any other speaker intending to communicate, wants to make herself understood, and she thus produces her utterance in such a way that she expects the hearer to be able to interpret it correctly. Nevertheless, irony cannot be too explicit, as this would spoil its true nature of indirectness. Let us notice that it would be very strange to start an ironic utterance with an explicit marker such as 'To speak ironically ...' or 'Ironically speaking ...', whereas it would be natural to introduce a metaphor by saying 'To speak metaphorically ...' or something to that effect.[6] Rather than ruining the irony with such a spoiler, the ironic speaker resorts to using subtler cues.

The speaker can use her voice as a clue for irony. We can say words with a tone that indicates to the audience that we are speaking ironically. This caused many authors to believe that there is a particular tone of voice that speakers use when being ironic – the 'ironic tone of voice'. This special tone of voice would be different from the tone a speaker uses when she is speaking literally.

The ironic tone of voice is generally described as an intonation with a lower pitch level, greater intensity and slower tempo than non-ironic, literal intonation. Several experiments tested and claimed to confirm the use of this type of intonation by ironic speakers.[7] Nevertheless, this position encounters two immediate obstacles.

---

[6] Grice (1967b/89: 54) previously warned us regarding this difference between metaphor and irony.

[7] See, for example, Rockwell (2000).

6.2 Traditional Clues
113

First, claims regarding the ironic tone of voice have been confusing and sometimes even contradictory.[8] This suggests that it is difficult to pinpoint this so-called ironic tone of voice, and we may even wonder whether it truly exists as a differentiated tone. Moreover, a number of experiments suggest that there may not be one particular tone of voice that ironic speakers use. Attardo et al. (2003), for instance, claim that there is no single tone of voice that could be called ironic but rather that ironic speakers tend to use such intonational patterns that contrast with the expected pattern or otherwise with the surrounding intonation. Similarly, Bryant and Fox Tree (2005) conclude that there is no such thing as an ironic tone of voice. Furthermore, Attardo et al. (2011) found that the difference in pitch between humorous (including ironic) and non-humorous turns was not significant in their experiments.

Summing up, there has been a generalized tendency to discuss the ironic speaker's particular tone of voice, but a lack of clarity and consensus weakens this position.

On a different note, some claim that what makes the tone of voice used when being ironic special is that it tends not to be the tone of voice that would typically accompany the literal utterance of such a sentence but the tone of voice corresponding to the attitude the speaker intends ultimately to communicate.

In this line, Grice, in his 'Further Notes on Logic and Conversation' (1967b/89: 53), wondered whether the speaker's tone of voice was not one of the elements missing in his succinct approach to irony, only to conclude speculating that this specific tone may not exist. Rather, he suggests that what we detect in ironic utterances is no more than the tone of voice connected with the attitude or feeling conveyed via the ironic remark. Similarly, Wilson and Sperber (2012: 143) explain that according to the echoic theory of irony, the tone of voice employed by an ironic speaker is a natural cue to the dissociative attitude the speaker is conveying.

In contrast, Clark and Gerrig (1984: 122) claim that the ironic speaker abandons her own voice and adopts the voice corresponding to who she is pretending to be. This is at odds with Grice's and Sperber and Wilson's position: while they claimed that the ironic speaker's tone of voice corresponds to the attitude she is conveying (that accompanies the implicit and ironic content of the utterance), Clark and

---

[8] In fact, the ironic tone of voice has been described as exhibiting either flat, rising or low pitch; see Attardo et al. (2003) for an extensive overview of the existing studies on the phonological markers of irony and sarcasm.

114   6 CLUES OF IRONY

Gerrig assert that the ironic speaker uses the tone of voice corresponding to the literal meaning of the utterance (that is, the tone of voice
that someone uttering the sentence literally would employ).

As a simple example, Mary, when ironically uttering, 'It's
a lovely day for a picnic, indeed', would use, according to Grice and
Sperber and Wilson, a mocking, scornful or complaining tone of
voice connected to the attitude she is conveying to Peter.
In contrast, according to Clark and Gerrig, Mary would use a happy,
complaisant or approving tone of voice connected to the literal
meaning of her utterance – or, as they would articulate it, connected
to the person she is pretending to be. Both scenarios initially appear
to be possible ways of being ironic. However, Wilson and Sperber
(2012: 142) settle the issue by clarifying that Clark and Gerrig are
correct when they observe that speakers, when being ironic, do
sometimes use the tone of voice that someone genuinely uttering
such a sentence would use (even exaggerating it), but this so is
because ironic speakers sometimes use a paroxdical tone of voice,
and it is exactly that tone which Clark and Gerrig describe – the tone
of voice corresponding to parody rather than to irony.

Among the cues of irony, the speaker's tone of voice has garnered
almost all the attention in the existing research. Other traditional
clues include the speaker's gestures or facial expressions and the use
of certain stylistic choices, such as hyperbole. Regarding the former,
little research has been conducted, aside from several experiments
suggesting that the so-called blank face may be a marker of ironic
intention.[9] Regarding the latter, it is interesting that irony and
hyperbole appear to co-occur. I develop this point in Section 6.3 as
I propose the view of hyperbole as a way of emphasizing the contradiction between meanings in irony.

6.3   OPPOSITION, ECHO AND PRETENCE

It is time for a brief recapitulation. In the first chapters of this book,
I focused on the main pragmatic theories that explain ironic communication. In subsequent chapters, I am focusing on several central
features of irony. I first presented the role of attitude expression in
ironic communication, and I will now elaborate on the clues ironic
speakers use.

---

[9] See Attardo et al. (2003) for results and discussion of this experiment, as well as for
    a review of the literature existing on this issue.

6.3 Opposition, Echo and Pretence   115

Let me introduce an important point here. When theorizing with regard to ironic communication, we must distinguish between two different (although related) explanatory tasks. First, we must answer the following question: what makes an utterance ironic? Then, we must attempt to solve the following puzzle: how do speakers actually communicate by being ironic? In the first case, one looks for what all ironic utterances have in common. In the second case, one attempts to clarify which strategies speakers use when uttering a sentence ironically.

The answer to the first question is allegedly provided by the theories I introduced in the first chapters. What makes an utterance ironic is that the speaker implicates the opposite (Grice), echoes (Sperber and Wilson) or pretends (Clark and Gerrig), along with the expression of a certain attitude. This chapter, in contrast, answers the second question. Speakers communicate ironically with the aid of particular clues.

I do not believe that this is an accurate picture, however. In this section, I claim that Grice, Sperber and Wilson, and Clark and Gerrig have sometimes confused these two explanatory tasks. More precisely, they have claimed that their theories offer an answer to what irony is, when, in fact, they explain how irony (typically) works. What I intend to suggest is that communicating the opposite meaning, echoing and pretending are three ways of being ironic rather than essential conditions for it. They should thus be compiled with the other clues of irony.

In the following pages I will show how these three features can work as clues in irony. In Section 6.4, I will explain how an account of irony would look if we accept that opposition, echo and pretence are just that: clues that ironic speakers may use to make themselves understood.

6.3.1 Opposition

Although the different accounts of irony offer diverse explanations for ironic communication, one thing appears to be established: there is always a clash in irony between what the speaker appears to be putting forward and what she actually intends to communicate (be it an implicature, an attitude towards an echoed thought or an attitude towards a pretended speaker). Thus, terminological issues aside, we may agree that what the speaker intends to communicate and what she appears to be putting forward are discordant.

The speaker, as she wants the hearer to correctly understand her utterance, wants him to recognize the discordance. One way to make

116 6 CLUES OF IRONY

that discordance clear is to exaggerate it; that is, the speaker can exaggerate the clash between what she is apparently saying and what she really intends to communicate. The largest discordance will be that found between two opposite contents. Thus, putting forward a literal meaning while intending to communicate just the opposite – irony's characteristic feature, according to the classical accounts and to Grice – can be considered a clue in irony, a clue that ironic speakers may and often do use to help hearers recognize the underlying clash.

It is at this point that the use of hyperbole finds its place. If the speaker's strategy is to exaggerate the clash between what she is putting forward and what she is intending to communicate, hyperbole can be of considerable help.[10]

Let us consider Sperber and Wilson's picnic example. If it is raining torrentially, it may be sufficiently clear for Mary to utter, 'It is a lovely day for a picnic', to make Peter understand that she is being ironic – contextual information helps substantially in this case. However, let us imagine that it is not actually raining but only cloudy and chilly – weather upon whose appropriateness for a picnic we may disagree but that Mary herself believes is certainly not suitable. In this context, if Mary utters, 'It is a lovely day for a picnic', Peter may have a problem detecting the irony, as he may believe that Mary actually thinks it is a lovely day to go for a picnic and is sincerely claiming so. In this situation, it would be safer for Mary to utter a sentence in which the clash between what she is apparently saying and what she is really attempting to communicate is more evident. To this end, Mary could use hyperbole:

(43)   Isn't it the loveliest day ever to go for a picnic?

(44)   I have never seen such a nice and lovely day for a picnic.

(45)   I am delighted that we can have a picnic just on the loveliest day ever.

---

[10] Kreuz and Roberts (1995) previously suggested the idea that hyperbole is related to exaggeration between one's apparent saying and the intended ironic interpretation. They satisfactorily tested this hypothesis with an experiment and observed that hyperbole can be a reliable clue for ironic interpretation. They went even farther and linked the alleged ironic tone of voice with the use of hyperbole: this tone of voice may be no more than the typical tone employed when uttering a hyperbole.

6.3 Opposition, Echo and Pretence

By exaggerating the distance between the literal meaning and what she intends to communicate, Mary makes it easier for Peter to recognize that what she is apparently saying cannot be what she really intends to communicate. To put forward the opposite of what one intends to communicate or to use hyperbole to emphasize this clash may be a useful clue when being ironic.

6.3.2 Echo

The role of the echo as a clue in irony is twofold. First, it plays the same role as traditional clues of irony. The ironic speaker does not put forward explicitly what she intends to communicate. Instead, she asks the hearer to make an effort and look for the ironic interpretation. Common knowledge and context can help both speaker and hearer succeed in this attempt. However, the speaker can also use signs to help the hearer in his effort. With the help of such clues, the hearer will recognize that the speaker is not *saying* what she appears to be saying. Echoing is one of the clues that the speaker can employ for this purpose – similarly to putting forward the opposite of what you intend to communicate. By recognizing that the speaker is echoing an identifiable utterance or thought, the hearer will understand that the speaker intended to achieve something 'special' with the utterance.

The incident involving the cover of *The New Yorker* can help us here. The illustrator did not portray the Obamas perpetrating any misdeed, and he did not randomly choose their attire. Barack and Michelle Obama were depicted with clothes and manners that linked them precisely to the criticisms that had been aired against them. As it had been claimed that he was a radical pro-Muslim, Barack was now wearing a turban. As she had been linked to the Black Panthers, Michelle now resembled one of them. According to the editor of the magazine, the aim of the illustrator had been to 'hold up a mirror' to all the bold accusations that the couple had had to endure during recent months. Using our terms, we would say that the author of the illustration was *echoing* those criticisms that he himself intended to ironically criticize. Readers were expected to be familiar with all that had been said about the Obamas, and recognizing those claims in the illustration may have helped them to understand the illustrator's ironic intentions.

The same occurs with echo used in verbal irony. Let us imagine again that Peter and Mary went for a picnic, and the day was cloudy and chilly. If Peter had said this morning that it would be a lovely day for a picnic, Mary can echo his exact words – instead of being ironic without repeating his words, as by uttering, 'How nice it is to shiver

118   6 CLUES OF IRONY

while eating a sandwich outdoors!' – and doing so, she will help Peter recognize her ironic intent.

Second, the echo can accomplish a mission that traditional clues cannot. We already know that the ironic speaker always expresses an attitude that is typically negative. The target of this attitude is called the 'victim' of the irony. One way of identifying this target may be to echo his words or thoughts. When the hearer recognizes the echo, he will be able to identify where this echo comes from; moreover, once he has detected the source, he will have no doubt regarding who the victim of the irony is. The echo thus may be the tell-tale clue of the ironic criticism.

Returning to the cloudy picnic, let us imagine now that Peter and Mary are accompanied by several friends who were not present when Peter said this morning that it was going to be a lovely day for a picnic. When Mary utters, 'It is a lovely day for a picnic', in this situation, different levels of understanding may occur. One friend may believe that she was speaking sincerely, as he himself likes cloudy days and has no reason to believe that Mary does not. Another friend may recognize that Mary is being ironic – because he knows Mary better and knows she hates cloudy days, for example – and understand that she is ironically complaining about the gloomy weather. However, Peter is the only one who can go farther: he recognizes that Mary is echoing his previous words, and thus he understands that (apart from complaining about the weather, maybe) she is mocking him with her irony.

Thus, the echo, as a clue for irony, can help the hearer realize that the speaker is not intending to communicate what she is putting forward, recognize what she intends to communicate and identify the victim of the irony. Echoing is a special clue because it is related to both crucial characteristics of irony: the discordance and the (negative) evaluative attitude. Thus, it should not surprise us to discover that it is one of the most frequent clues of irony and that certain examples appear to rely on it heavily.

This approach to the concept of the echo allows us to preserve the original and strongest notion of it. Echoing is repeating an openly identifiable utterance or thought. We must only accept that it is not something that we find in every ironic utterance, although we do find it in many.

6.3.3 Pretence

The role of pretence in irony can be explained in similar terms. We have observed that defining the meaning of pretence is not an easy endeavour, and authors appear to disagree with regard to this

6.4 A Minimal Account of Irony 119

definition even when they agree with the claim that the ironic speaker pretends.

In a sense, we can assume that pretending is similar to displaying a certain tone of voice, gestures and expressions that can be recognized as pertaining to a more or less identifiable source. Thus, for example, Mary can imitate Peter's voice and mimic a gesture typical of him when ironically uttering, 'It is a lovely day for a picnic, indeed!', or maybe she can make as if she was a happy person enjoying the rainy weather, skipping and happily uttering, 'It is a lovely day for a picnic, indeed!'.

Pretence, considered thus, is no more than a mixture of irony's traditional clues or signals. When discussing irony, pretending would be the act of using certain clues to emphasize the underlying clash. In so doing, the speaker can help the hearer recognize that she is intending to communicate something different from the literal meaning of the utterance to help him recover the ironic interpretation and to indicate the victim of the negative attitude expressed via irony simply by pretending to be that victim.

6.4 A MINIMAL ACCOUNT OF IRONY

Echo, pretence and opposition have been introduced as defining notions of irony. Ironic communication has been claimed to be based on each of these concepts and thus to be explainable in terms of each one, respectively. As a consequence, these theories have defended that there is no irony without echo, pretence or opposition. In the preceding section, in contrast, I have shown that echo, pretence and opposition can be viewed as clues of irony – not necessary elements for being ironic but indeed typical and useful for ironic communication. I have thus suggested that echo, pretence and irony do not explain what irony is but rather how irony is typically communicated.

Echo, pretence and opposition fit well within the list of ironic clues. However, of course, I have a strong motivation for claiming that they should be considered as clues and not as essential or defining for irony. In the first chapters of this book, I addressed the main pragmatic accounts of irony (which are based on these very three notions that I am now calling into question). I noted that they all have several weaknesses or limitations, one of which is common to all three: there are instances of irony that are difficult to explain in terms of echo, pretence or opposition.

120   6 CLUES OF IRONY

When confronted with these problematic examples, the theories do not have an easy solution. The idea of the echo, for instance, could be broadened and weakened to apply it to these varied cases of irony. This appears to be, in fact, the strategy of the echoic account. The same could most likely be accomplished with the notion of pretence or with the view of irony as the communication of the opposite. However, what I want to defend here is a different position. There are indeed many cases in which a speaker is ironic and pretends, echoes or implicates the opposite. However, what occurs in all cases of irony is something more basic. What unites all cases of irony is that the speaker puts forward content that clashes with what she actually intends to communicate, and she does so overtly – meaning that the speaker intends the hearer to recognize both the clash and the intention to make it recognizable.

When a speaker is ironic, the literal meaning of her utterance is discordant with the belief that she actually intends to communicate – the belief which critical pragmatics and the *asif*-theory call the speaker's 'motivating belief'. We will always find that clash in an ironic utterance. We will find it in the examples introduced by Grice, Clark and Gerrig and Sperber and Wilson because every time we say that a speaker makes as if to say something she believes to be false, or echoes something that she attributes to someone else (or to herself at another time), or pretends to say something without saying it, we are already accepting that a clash between contents underlies that utterance. There are indeed no cases in which the speaker flouts the maxim of quality, echoes an attributed thought or pretends to say something in which we will not find a clash between what the speaker intends to communicate and what she appears to be putting forward. Thus, the examples introduced in the accounts I have reviewed here can easily be explained by my proposal. More than that, even in the examples that the three accounts struggled to explain, we find a clash between contents.

Grice claimed that every time a speaker is ironic, she intends to communicate the opposite meaning of that which she makes as if to say. Therefore, cases in which no opposite is communicated constituted the clearest problem for him. I am referring to this type of case:

> During the precept, Danny was dominating the discussion. He certainly seemed to be familiar with the subject, but he was obnoxious in the way he showed off his knowledge. Jesse, one of Danny's classmates, said:

6.4 A Minimal Account of Irony 121

(5) You sure know a lot.

(Kumon-Namakura et al. 1995: 7)

Bill is a neurotically cautious driver who keeps his petrol tank full, never fails to indicate when turning and repeatedly scans the horizon for possible dangers. His companion says:

(6) I really appreciate cautious drivers.

(Wilson 2006: 1726)

A mother says to her teenage son:

(7) I love children who keep their rooms clean,

just as she has discovered that her son, once again, failed to clean his room.

(Gibbs & O'Brien 1991: 525)

In the first example, in which Danny was behaving obnoxiously, the hearers recognize that Jesse is not (or not primarily) communicating that Danny knows a lot – even if he does actually believe that Danny knows a lot. Thus, there is an obvious clash between what Jesse appears to be putting forward (that Danny knows a lot) and what he intends to communicate with the ironic utterance (that Danny is arrogant and pretentious, for example). The same occurs in the example of the cautious driver: Bill can easily see that the speaker, even if he may actually like cautious drivers, is not primarily intending to communicate that when uttering **(6)**. Similarly, the children realize that their mother is not primarily communicating that she loves clean children but that she is disappointed with their messy room. In all of these cases, the literal meanings of the utterances clash with the beliefs that the speakers are actually intending to communicate, and the hearers can recognize that overt clash. In fact, only if they do recognize that overt clash will they be able to grasp the intended irony.

In the examples that were problematic for the echoic account, a similar clash can be found. Let us recall one of these examples:

Mary and someone she does not know are waiting for the elevator after having left a funeral. It has been long and boring – as funerals are expected to be in their shared culture. Mary says:

(20) That was fun!

122 6 CLUES OF IRONY

Someone who, after a funeral, hears Mary's utterance, **(20)** 'That was fun!', may not understand that she is being ironic because he perceives **(20)** as echoing a widely shared expectation that events should be fun – as the defenders of the echoic account would claim. What he *does* perceive is the discordance between what Mary is apparently claiming and what she may presumably be intending to communicate: the hearer recognizes that Mary, even if she believes that the funeral was as boring as could have been expected, has still apparently said that it was fun, and it is because the hearer recognizes this contradiction – and also recognizes that Mary has intended for him to recognize both the discordance and the intention to make it recognizable – that he understands that Mary has been ironic. An overt discordance between what the speaker believes and what she is apparently saying – combined with a certain attitude of mockery, annoyance or complaint – is sufficient for a hearer to understand the irony in this example.

It is more difficult to agree on which are real counter-examples to the pretence theory – because that depends on the notion of pretence we would like to hold, and it is not very clear what precise notion that is in the case of Clark and Gerrig's pretence theory. However, if pretending is playing someone else's role and demonstrating that one is doing so, the following could count as a candidate:

> Jaime and Lu go to Hawaii on their honeymoon. They had dreamed about sunny weather and the beach. Unfortunately, the weather was terrible during their stay. It did not stop raining, it was awfully windy and they even had a hurricane. The day they came back home, Christina picks them up at the airport. They are pale, and they look tired, frustrated and angry. Christina asks politely, 'So, how was Hawaii?' Jaime replies dryly:

(46) Wonderful.

We may agree that claiming that Jaime is pretending, playing the fool, showing purposely affected ignorance or playing make-believe appears forced here. Christina will be able to recognize that he is speaking ironically regardless. She did not recognize it because of Jaime's pretence but because she can grasp that Jaime is not intending to communicate what he appears to be putting forward – that their honeymoon was wonderful. This slight clash is the element that makes this utterance, as well as all the utterances we have considered so far, ironic.

6.4 A Minimal Account of Irony

All the examples I have presented thus far rely on an overt clash between contents: those which were presented as clear instances of echoic irony, pretence-based ironic cases or instances of irony based on an opposition between meanings, along with those which were difficult to explain based on the ideas of echo, pretence and opposition. An overt clash between contents is something we will find in every ironic utterance.

My proposal is thus as follows: instead of attempting to accommodate the strong notions of echo, opposition and pretence into the vast variety of ironic examples, let us accept that what unites all instances of irony is something more basic – an overt clash between contents. The concepts that other theories have situated at the core of ironic communication are actually important in irony. Pretence, echo and opposition do play a significant role in irony. These approaches were correct in this respect; they simply failed to realize that these three features, although important, are not essential to irony.

In the preceding section I presented an alternative analysis of echo, pretence and opposition in which they are treated as the means of expressing ironic content. Moreover, in Chapter 5, I claimed that irony is essentially negative. Combining these two claims into a humble and basic pragmatic conception of irony can result in a general and sufficient characterization of it.

From this position, I have no trouble accepting that ironic utterances can adopt a wide variety of different patterns and that irony can be expressed in many different and varied forms. What unites all instances of irony, what is essential and basic for ironic communication, is something simple and basic: an overt clash between what the speaker intends to communicate and what she is apparently putting forward, along with the expression of a negative attitude. This is something that will be found underlying every ironic utterance; it answers what irony *is*. Additionally, due to its artful peculiarities, irony is a tool that should be used with care; thus, there is a way in which we are ironic. Ironic speakers typically use clues, such as a particular tone of voice, hyperbole emphasizing the ironic clash, an echo repeating a familiar source or a recognizable pretence. These features explain *how* we speak ironically.

This account must be refined and elaborated – I have already provided hints in the papers listed below under 'Suggested Reading'. However, I believe that by considering echo, opposition and pretence as three compatible means of expression that are typical of ironic communication, we will be able to offer a more complete analysis of the varied and rich expressions of verbal irony.

6.5 SUGGESTED READING

6.5.1 Risks and Benefits of Irony

Gibbs and Colston analyze how irony can affect the relationship between speaker and hearer. Their aim is to explain *why* we decide to use irony even if it is a risky way to communicate.

Gibbs, R. W. & H. L. Colston. 2001. The risks and rewards of ironic communication. In *Say Not to Say: New Perspectives on Miscommunication*, ed. L. Anolli, R. Ciceri & G. Riva, 187–200. Amsterdam: IOS Press.

6.5.2 Traditional Clues

Here Muecke presents a general list of irony markers, with beautiful examples from literary texts. He divides irony markers into kinesic, graphic, phonic, lexical and discourse markers.

Muecke, D. 1978. Irony markers. *Poetics* 7: 363–75.

Attardo and colleagues offer elaborate reviews of the existing literature regarding the use of markers in irony, along with a number of interesting experiments and discussions. The following two articles may be most suitable to approach their view:

Attardo, S., J. Eisterhold, J. Hay & I. Poggi. 2003. Multimodal markers of irony and sarcasm. *Humor* 16(2): 243–60.
Attardo, S., L. Pickering & A. Baker. 2011. Prosodic and multimodal markers of humor in conversation. *Pragmatics & Cognition* 19(2): 224–47.

To acquaint yourself with the disagreements regarding the issue of the ironic speaker's tone of voice, you can peruse two already classic articles, each concluding in a different direction.

Bryant, G. A. & J. E. Fox Tree. 2005. Is there an ironic tone of voice? *Language and Speech* 48(3): 257–77.
Rockwell, P. 2000. Lower, slower, louder: vocal cues of sarcasm. *Journal of Psycholinguistic Research* 29(5): 483–95.

Carston and Wearing's article focuses on analyzing hyperbole but also touches on its relationship with ironic language. The second paper examines the role of hyperbole in irony and suggests an alternative explanation of the ironic speaker's tone of voice.

6.5 Suggested Reading

Carston, R. & C. Wearing. 2015. Hyperbolic language and its relation to metaphor and irony. *Journal of Pragmatics* 79: 79–92.

Kreuz, R. J. & R. M. Roberts. 1995. Two cues for verbal irony: hyperbole and the ironic tone of voice. *Metaphor and Symbolic Activity* 10(1): 21–31.

6.5.3 A Minimal Account of Irony

I have introduced the basics of my proposal in the following articles:

Garmendia, J. 2010. Irony is critical. *Pragmatics and Cognition* 18(2): 397–421.

Garmendia, J. 2011. She's (not) a fine friend: 'saying' and criticism in irony. *Intercultural Pragmatics* 8(1): 41–65.

Garmendia, J. 2013. Ironically saying and implicating. In *What Is Said and What Is Not: The Semantics/Pragmatics Interface*, eds. C. Penco & F. Domaneschi, 225–41. Stanford: CSLI Publications.

Garmendia, J. 2014. The clash: humor and critical attitude in verbal irony. *Humor* 27(4): 641–59.

Garmendia, J. 2015. A (neo-)Gricean account of irony: an answer to relevance theory. *International Review of Pragmatics* 7: 40–79.

7 Sarcasm and Humour

Thus far, my aim has been to shed light on what irony is and how irony works in communication. After a brief clarification regarding the different types of irony, I focused on explaining the characteristics of verbal irony from a pragmatic standpoint. First, I introduced the main theories of irony that attempt to explain how ironic communication is carried out. Then I touched on two fundamental features of irony: the (typically negative) attitude expressed by ironic speakers and the means of expression they commonly use. Presently, it is time to broaden our investigative horizon and focus on two notions that are related to irony on different levels: in this chapter, I will explain the relationship between irony and both sarcasm and humour.

Up to this point, I have discussed irony as if it were a notion that is easy to delimitate or as if ironic cases constituted a clearly defined set. I have done so for the sake of argument, but in truth, I have intentionally ignored certain tensions that inevitably appear anytime we address this subject. We all refer to irony as if we share a clear idea of what it is, but then we may not easily agree regarding whether a certain case is in fact irony or maybe sarcasm, parody, a witty joke and so on.

Among the cases that typically mingle with irony and blur its boundaries, sarcasm is remarkably the most problematic one. Thus far, I have used 'irony' as an umbrella term – as if it were a general term that covers all sarcastic/ironic cases. It is now time to set the record straight and finally clarify how irony and sarcasm relate to each other. I do so in Section 7.1.

Another issue that I have not addressed up to this moment is the role of humour in verbal irony. Humour is an extensive phenomenon, and it ranges far beyond irony. However, it also appears that it plays a particular role in ironic communication, whatever that may be. I address this issue in Section 7.2.

7.1 Irony and Sarcasm

7.1 IRONY AND SARCASM

Explaining ironic communication has traditionally been a challenge for pragmatic theories: understanding how speakers communicate by being ironic will help to explain how human communication works overall. Sarcasm has typically played a supporting role on the pragmatic scene: the main purpose of analyzing sarcasm has been to shed light on the study of irony. Thus, analyses of sarcasm have traditionally been an appendix to theories of irony.

> **Etymology**
> The word 'sarcasm' originates from the Greek σαρκασμός (*sarkasmos*), which is taken from σαρκάζειν, meaning 'to tear flesh, bite the lip in rage, sneer'.

Irony and sarcasm appear inevitably bound to each other in the field of pragmatics. Nonetheless, the relationship between the two phenomena remains unclear. Here I will map the main lines of this debate. We should bear in mind, however, that this theoretical debate is based on a pre-theoretical confusion: the distinction between irony and sarcasm is unclear among natural speakers, and the differences are accentuated when we compare different cultures or linguistic communities.

For example, in Chapter 1, I used an example from the TV series *The Big Bang Theory* in which Kripke says to Leonard:

(47)   Heard about your latest anti-proton decay experiment. 20,000 data runs and no statistically significant results. Very impressive.

I introduced this example as an instance of verbal irony, and it appears that it would easily be accommodated within the theories of irony we have considered thus far, as it straightforwardly parallels many of the examples that are acknowledged as ironic. However, I wonder whether the characters in the series (or indeed the scriptwriters) would not call this a sarcastic remark. In fact, most of the instances in which someone makes a mocking, indirect and sometimes funny comment in the series, it is called sarcasm, as, for example, in the following dialogue between Penny and Sheldon, in which Penny has asked Sheldon for help (*The Big Bang Theory*, Season 2, Episode 18):

> SHELDON: Just to be clear here, you are asking for my assistance.
> PENNY: Yes.
> SHELDON: And you understand that will involve me telling you what to do?

128   7 SARCASM AND HUMOUR

PENNY: I understand.
SHELDON: And you are not allowed to be sarcastic or snide to
   me while I am doing so.
PENNY: Okay.
SHELDON: Good. Let us begin with the premise that everything
   you have done up to this point is wrong.
PENNY: Oh, imagine that.
SHELDON: Sarcasm. Good-bye.
PENNY: No, sorry. Wait! Please come back!

'Sarcasm' and 'sarcastic' are easily interchangeable with 'irony' and
'ironic' in this scene, in the sense in which I have employed the notion
of irony thus far. However, 'sarcasm' is used as the umbrella term in
this TV series – as I have used 'irony' up to now in this book. Rather
than a simple anecdote in a particular TV series, it appears that this
case illustrates a tendency that is becoming generalized in the United
States, which is to consider sarcasm as a broader concept than irony or
to call sarcasm what may be called irony in other cultures (and in the
United States itself until recently).[1] This tendency in a particular time
and language community illustrates a broader and more general
confusion that affects the use of the notions of sarcasm and irony in
different linguistic cultures or at different times.

The same confusion affects the issue on a theoretical level. Among
the authors working on pragmatics, verbal irony is typically used as
the general term, and sarcasm is considered to be closely related to it
but somehow distinguishable. However, exceptions do exist. Elisabeth
Camp (2012), for instance, attempts to explain the traditional
examples of verbal irony with a theory of sarcasm, although she
acknowledges the diversity of opinion existing on this issue and
admits that sarcasm may be a more restricted case than verbal irony.
Sky McDonald also attempts to offer an analysis of sarcasm, but if we
examine the definition she offers of sarcasm, we note that it is an
extremely similar definition to the one traditionally offered for irony:

> When a speaker makes a sarcastic comment, this is frequently in the
> form of an assertion that contradicts the true state of affairs. Sarcastic

---

[1] 'A shift in meaning for the word irony seems to be taking place with "sarcasm"
occupying what was previously the semantic space of "irony"' (Attardo et al. 2003:
243). Nunberg (2001: 91–93) addresses this fact in his compilation of 'Word Histories'.
Dynel (2016: 227) also mentions the semantic shift that is becoming noticeable in
American English, and she adds that a similar problem can be found in the Polish
language.

7.1 Irony and Sarcasm

comments are also normally associated with an attitude of derision or scorn toward the recipient of the comment. (McDonald 2000: 85)

There are also those who suggest that sarcasm and irony are interchangeable notions, such as Kendall Walton, who claims that 'to speak ironically is to mimic or mock those one disagrees with, fictionally to assert what they do or may assert. Irony is sarcasm' (Walton 1990: 222).

However, controversies aside, most authors agree that sarcasm and irony, although closely related, are not interchangeable; that is, they are two distinguishable phenomena. Most authors mention victims, aggressiveness and clarity when distinguishing between irony and sarcasm.

Sarcasm Is Always Verbal

When we compare irony and sarcasm and discuss their differences and similarities, we are actually comparing sarcasm and *verbal* irony. Indeed, as I noted in Chapter 1, irony can also be situational or dramatic. Sarcasm cannot. We do not say regarding an event or a situation that it was sarcastic. Sarcasm is only observed as a linguistic manifestation, which is why it can only be compared with linguistic, communicative irony – with verbal irony.

Activity 7.1A Irony and Sarcasm

I will touch on the differences between irony and sarcasm in the following subsections, but let us first test your intuitions. Here are two interesting examples:

The Orchid

Mary is worried because she received an orchid as a present, and after two days it already looks very withered.

> MARY: Oh, my poor orchid! Do you think it is dying?
> PETER: Oh, don't worry. I am sure it is only pretending to be dead. It just wants your attention; you know how orchids are.

The Girl

In a magazine, there is a picture that shows the corpse of a Palestinian girl and many adults trying to dig her out from the rubble of her house. Below the picture, we can read:

130   7 SARCASM AND HUMOUR

> "Here you have an anti-Semitic girl, letting herself be photographed, totally dead, with the sole aim of calling into question Israel's right to defend itself."[2]
>
> 1. Would you say that these examples are ironic or sarcastic?
> 2. How are the two examples similar?
> 3. How are they different?

7.1.1 Victims

First, according to many authors, the victims will enable us to distinguish irony from sarcasm. Irony is, at least typically, negative. The speaker, by being ironic, shows a negative attitude, typically implicit behind an apparent positive attitude. In this context, the target of the negative attitude will be the one we call the 'victim' of the ironic statement.

However, the target of irony's negative attitude is not always of the same type, as we have sensed in the variety of examples considered thus far. Sometimes the speaker criticizes herself, as when Asterios Polyp, the main character in David Mazzucchelli's graphic novel, mocks his deficient sex life:

> (48) Me? I like wearing a condom. It means I'm having sex. I already spend most of my time *not* wearing one. It's like a tuxedo – I enjoy putting one on for special occasions.
>
> (Mazzucchelli 2009: 57)

At other times, the target of the negative attitude is the audience, or someone in the audience, as with utterances **(7)**, **(15)** and **(35)**:

> A mother says to her teenage son:
>
> (7) I love children who keep their rooms clean,
>
> just as she has discovered that her son, once again, failed to clean his room.
>
> (Gibbs & O'Brien 1991: 525)

> PETER: It's a lovely day for a picnic.
>
> They go for a picnic and it rains.
>
> MARY (sarcastically):

---

[2] 'He aquí una niña antisemita en el instante de dejarse fotografiar, completamente muerta, con el único objeto de poner en duda el derecho de Israel a defenderse' (Juan José Millás, 'Demagogia', in *El País Semanal*, 3 January 2009).

7.1 *Irony and Sarcasm* 131

(15) It's a lovely day for a picnic, indeed.

(Sperber & Wilson 1986/95: 239)

(35) How about another small slice of pizza?
to someone who has just gobbled up the whole pie.

(Kumon-Nakamura et al. 1995: 4)

There are also ironic cases where the target of the criticism is a particular person identifiable by the audience but who is not in the audience himself, as in the following examples:

X, with whom A has been on close terms until now, has betrayed a secret of A's to a business rival. A and his audience both know this. A says:

(3) X is a fine friend.

(Grice 1967a/89: 34)

S U E (pointing to Jack, who has become a total nuisance after drinking some wine):

(16) As they say, a glass of wine is good for you!

(Wilson & Sperber 2012: 130)

(27) Jones, this murderer, this thief, this crook, is indeed an honourable fellow!

(Sperber 1984: 33)

Finally, there are also cases in which the negative attitude has a more general target and is directed towards a broad general audience or towards a non-human target, such as the weather, a country, an army and so on:

(28) Outside temperature is again below freezing point: a true heat wave!

(Sperber 1984: 33)

(49) America's allies – always there when they need you.

(Kaufer 1981: 501)

(50) Both the Penguins and the Porpoises had the most powerful army in the world.

(Zalecki 1990: 128; attributed by the author to Anatole France)

I suggest that these different targets may be arranged in descending order of closeness to the speaker, and this gradation will be among the

132   7 SARCASM AND HUMOUR

features that enable us to distinguish sarcasm from irony. Thus, the closest target of the ironic utterance would be the addressee; then, someone who is present in the audience; next, a clear target who is not present; and finally, a general target that cannot be easily identified.[3] It may also be the case that the criticism in an ironic utterance has a 'mixed' target: a concrete third-party hearer and a broader, more general and unspecified audience can both share criticism, for example.

The closer the victim is to the speaker, the more clearly targeted the negative attitude will be. Furthermore, sarcasm has as a distinguishing feature that its victims tend to be of the clearest type. Furthermore, instances of sarcasm will typically have a particular victim (instead of a general one), and this particular victim will, more often than not, be present.

Wilson frames the issue in a similar way. She states that 'verbal irony (and sarcasm in particular) often has a specific "target" or "victim"' (Wilson 2013: 43).

> Although the ironical attitude is directly targeted at attributed thoughts, it may be indirectly targeted (particularly in sarcasm) at specific people, or types of people, who entertain such thoughts or take them seriously, and in those cases it may be perceived as hurtful or mean. (Wilson 2013: 47)

For other authors, victims play a different role in the distinction between sarcasm and irony. For example, Sperber and Wilson claim that the 'mention' (the initial key concept of these authors' theory of irony) will help us to find this victim; the victim will be the person whose words the speaker mentions. If the victim is the speaker, it will be a case of 'self-directed' irony, and if the victim is the hearer, it will be a case of sarcasm (Sperber & Wilson 1981: 314).

However, according to McDonald (1999) and Kreuz & Glucksberg (1989), the difference is not whether the victim is the hearer or the speaker. Instead, merely having a victim is sufficient to consider an utterance to be an example of sarcasm.

Summing up, in one way or another, many authors regard victims as a factor distinguishing between sarcasm and irony. This agreement is deceptive, however: the role victims play in this issue is understood differently by the different approaches. If we look for areas of agreement, I would say that the tendency is to consider sarcasm typically to have a victim, this victim typically to be easily identifiable and even for

---

[3] Cases where the speaker criticizes herself are challenging to place in this gradation. It may be that self-criticisms are typically not as severe as criticism originating from someone else.

7.1 Irony and Sarcasm 133

the victim typically to be present or to be the direct addressee of the utterance. However, many shades and variations exist in this respect, as I have illustrated.

7.1.2 Aggressiveness

The second feature that invariably appears when listing the differences between irony and sarcasm is bitterness or aggressiveness: sarcasm is often said to be particularly hurtful.

I have repeatedly noted that irony is acknowledged to always express an attitude that is typically negative. Thus, irony is generally used to criticize, complain or mock. When being ironic, a speaker can express a wide array of negatively evaluative attitudes: in verbal irony, the speaker can criticize, complain, discredit, mock and so on. Furthermore, depending on the attitude that the speaker has expressed, irony can be used for either gentle or sharp criticism.

Thus, the negative attitude communicated by the ironic speaker can be more or less aggressive. Scorning a friend for having been disloyal (as in **(3)**), criticizing a friend for his lack of personality **(51)**, teasing a friend for his gluttony **(35)** and mocking a friend's mistaken prediction of the weather **(18)** are all ways of expressing a negatively evaluative attitude towards a friend, but they do not appear to be equally hurtful, pointed or unkind:

> X, with whom A has been on close terms until now, has betrayed a secret of A's to a business rival. A and his audience both know this. A says:

> (3) X is a fine friend.

> (Grice 1967a/89: 34)

> (51) Wait, I'm trying to imagine you with a personality.

> (35) How about another small slice of pizza?

> to someone who has just gobbled up the whole pie.

> (Kumon-Nakamura et al. 1995: 4)

> Nancy and her friend Jane were planning a trip to the beach.
> 'The weather should be nice tomorrow', said Jane, who worked for a local TV station as a meteorologist.
> The next day was a cold and stormy one.
> As she looked out of the window, Nancy said:

> (18) This certainly is beautiful weather.

> (Wilson & Sperber 2012: 128)

134   7 SARCASM AND HUMOUR

The differences among the attitudes conveyed appear to play a role when differentiating between irony and sarcasm. While the negative attitude can vary from mild to sharp, sarcasm is said to convey the sharpest, bitterest and most hurtful type of negative attitude. This is something that is unanimously accepted, even if not all authors use the same terminology.[4] However, overall, they all appear to point in the same direction: in both sarcasm and irony, the speaker expresses a typically negative attitude, which can vary in the degree of bitterness, and examples of sarcasm typically convey attitudes at the sharpest end.

7.1.3 Clarity

There is also a third feature that is commonly viewed as significant when trying to distinguish between irony and sarcasm: sarcastic cases are viewed as clearer, more explicit or more direct than ironic ones. In other words, sarcasm would leave no room for doubt regarding the speaker's intended meaning. Thus, sarcasm would not be able to backtrack – it is not as slippery as irony. This characteristic has been named in different ways; Barbe, for example, asserts that sarcasm is *stable*:

> What makes it sarcasm, however, is that the interpretation of the ironic utterance *has to be* ironic-sarcastic, it is thus somewhat stable. Speakers cannot later say *I did not mean it* in an attempt to save face because sarcasm leaves no room for guessing or doubting, for the so-called benefit of doubt, which may be found in other non-sarcastic instances of irony. (Barbe 1995: 29)

I explained the risks of being ironic in Chapter 6. Ironic cases can be uncertain because they can easily mislead the audience. This uncertainty is produced by irony's implicitness; the speaker does not directly put forward what she intends to communicate, but she does it indirectly (by making as if to say the literal meaning, by echoing it or by pretending to say it, according to the main theories of irony). This is where irony's most dangerous risk arises: because the hearer may understand the speaker to have spoken non-ironically, and thus, he

---

[4] For example, Haiman regards sarcasm as a form of irony used as verbal *aggression* (Haiman 1998: 20); Gibbs & Colston (2001: 190) and Kumon-Nakamura et al. (1995: 4, note 1) call sarcasm *hurtful*; Muecke asserts that sarcasm is the *crudest* form of irony (Muecke 1969: 54), and Camp (2012: 603) explains that sarcasm is typically considered to be more *pointed* and *negative* than irony.

7.1 Irony and Sarcasm   135

can eventually ask her to take responsibility for believing in the truth of something that she did not actually intend to communicate.

I have also explained that the ironic speaker can use different techniques to avoid misunderstandings. There are certain distinctive means of expression of irony, such as the speaker's tone of voice and others that could also be included in this traditional list, such as pretence, contradiction and echo. These resources are available to the ironic speaker, but she does not necessarily have to use them. In fact, this is one of the main particularities of irony. It is said that irony's greatest charm, at least stylistically, lies in its being clear as mud.

Furthermore, the difference between certain ironic cases and others depends precisely on this choice: the ironic speaker can use certain clues and means of expression to make her intentions completely clear. However, she can also hide these intentions, thus camouflaging the path to the content that she intends to communicate. The speaker can even make it particularly difficult for the hearer to realize that she is being ironic. As a result, certain ironic cases are much clearer, more obvious, blatant and more direct than others.

Let me revisit examples of the two extremes: one with clear clues and the other one with no clue at all:

> PETER: It's a lovely day for a picnic.
>
> They go for a picnic and it rains.
>
> MARY (sarcastically[5]):
>
> (15) It's a lovely day for a picnic, indeed.
>
> (Sperber & Wilson 1986/95: 239)

In this example, the speaker uses the typical resources of irony to point to what she intends to communicate: the utterance is an echo (a verbatim repetition) of Peter's utterance of this morning, and the literal meaning of the utterance is also the opposite of what the speaker is actually intending to communicate. Apart from these two clues, we may assume that the speaker also used many others to make her utterance's irony even more obvious. She may have used a special tone of voice or may have shown the hearer that she was being ironic by making certain gestures, for example.

The following example is different in this respect:

---

[5] Sperber and Wilson say 'sarcastically' here, as do I, but with no intention of making a point with regard to the issue I am elaborating.

136   7 SARCASM AND HUMOUR

During the precept, Danny was dominating the discussion. He certainly seemed to be familiar with the subject, but he was obnoxious in the way he showed off his knowledge. Jesse, one of Danny's classmates, said:

(5) You sure know a lot.

     (Kumon-Namakura et al. 1995: 7)

In contrast to the preceding example, in this case, the speaker has not used either contradiction or echo as a clue. Supposing that, in addition, he has not used a specific tone of voice, made gestures or provided any other clue, this would be a case of the subtlest form of irony. In fact, the only way to realize that Jesse is being ironic is to notice that he does not really want to communicate what he appears to be putting forward; however, the hearer does not have any specific clue to do so – nevertheless, irony can work in this instance as well.

Thus, ironic cases can vary noticeably in clarity. This feature is, as I have mentioned, the third element that is often listed as a distinguishing feature between sarcasm and irony – sarcasm would be on the clearer and more explicit end.[6]

7.1.4 Summary

I have attempted to compile here the basics of the debate on the relationship between irony and sarcasm. Nevertheless, you may still have the impression that there is not sufficient light on the matter. This is a complex issue, and as I have noted, there is no minimum consensus regarding how irony and sarcasm are related: they are claimed both to be interchangeable notions and completely different concepts; sarcasm is said to be a type of irony, and vice versa. There are also those who use the two labels without much rigour. Finally, if this were not sufficient, this theoretical and terminological chaos is built upon an inconsistent use of the terms by natural speakers.

I have attempted to gather the basic elements that are most often repeated when addressing this issue. While the relationship between sarcasm and irony is not clear and agreed upon, at least the predominant view considers them to be different to a certain extent. Furthermore, although the differences between the two notions are explained differently in the diverse approaches, at least there are certain features that appear with a certain frequency. Three characteristics are commonly used to distinguish sarcasm from irony. As Attardo correctly summarizes, 'Sarcasm is an overtly *aggressive*

---

[6] Attardo (2000); Barbe (1995); Camp (2012).

7.1 Irony and Sarcasm

type of irony, with *clearer* markers/cues and a clear target' (Attardo 2000: 795, my emphasis).

This minimum consensus still leaves too many loose ends. Are there any parameters by which we can discern whether an instance belongs to either side of the spectrum? Are irony and sarcasm two sides of the same coin, or does one encompass the other? There is not, to my knowledge, a fully elaborated answer to these questions that stands out from the other possible positions.

Activity 7.1B Irony and Sarcasm

Let us return to the examples I presented in Activity 7.1A. Which intuitions did you have then? Did you think one of the cases was sarcasm and the other irony?

Read the examples again, and attempt to test them according to the elements I just introduced.

The Orchid

Mary is worried because she received an orchid as a present and after two days it already looks very withered.

> MARY: Oh, my poor orchid! Do you think it is dying?
> PETER: Oh, don't worry. I am sure it is only pretending to be dead. It just wants your attention; you know how orchids are.

The Girl

In a magazine, there is a picture that shows the corpse of a Palestinian girl and many adults trying to dig her out from the rubble of her house. Below the picture, we can read:

"Here you have an anti-Semitic girl, letting herself be photographed, totally dead, with the sole aim of calling into question Israel's right to defend itself."

1. Do both examples have an identifiable victim? What type of victim is it?
2. Would you say that one of the examples is more bitter, crude or aggressive than the other?
3. Are the examples equally clear? Can you identify clues of irony/sarcasm in either of them?
4. Does one of the examples show more of the features that are commonly associated with sarcasm? Does the result coincide with your first intuitions?

---

138   7 SARCASM AND HUMOUR

7.2 *IRONY AND HUMOUR*

Irony and humour are frequently claimed to be related. Irony is often funny, as typically acknowledged among natural speakers.[7] In this section, I present two of the main conceptions of humour and show how they can help us to explain the links between ironic communication and humorousness.

Humour has been analyzed extensively, both within and outside the linguistic field. Different theories of verbal humour have been presented and discussed, and the debate on the essentials of linguistic humour has developed visibly over the last decades. My aim here is not to delve deeply into the theories of humour per se. A comprehensive and developed work on humorous meanings can be found in the collection by Andrew Goatly (2012), and at the end of this section, I will provide further readings related to the study of humour as well. In the following pages, I will briefly present two of the main approaches to verbal humour – the superiority and incongruity theories – to determine how they can explain the connections between humour and irony.

7.2.1 Superiority Theories of Humour

It may sound surprising from our current perspective, but for centuries laughter and humour were not very highly regarded. In search of the roots of this view, we can go as far back as Plato's *Philebus* and Aristotle's *Poetics*.

However, it was Thomas Hobbes who articulated these ideas into what could be considered the first version of a theory that was later called the 'superiority theory of humour'. In his work *Leviathan*, Hobbes described human beings as individualistic and competitive, absorbed by a constant tension to win or lose. In this context, any sign that we are winning, any feeling of superiority, may result in laughter. This account has been associated with the idea of 'sudden glory'.

> The passion of laughter is nothing else but sudden glory arising from some sudden conception of some eminency in ourselves, by comparison with the infirmity of others, or with our own formerly. (Hobbes, *Human Nature*, chap. IX, 13)

---

[7] And corroborated by empirical studies, such as Dews et al. (1995); Kreuz et al. (1991); Kumon-Nakamura et al. (1995); Matthews et al. (2006); Toplak & Katz (2000).

7.2 *Irony and Humour* 139

Thus, simply stated, laughter arises when we feel superior to others. This summarizes Hobbes' superiority theory of humour – or of laughter, as it has often been correctly noted. Different approaches expanded this basic idea into more developed proposals focusing on superiority as fundamental for humour and laughter.[8]

Here are several classical examples of superiority-based jokes[9]:

BLONDE: What does IDK stand for?
BRUNETTE: I don't know.
BLONDE: OMG, nobody does!

Two blondes fell down a hole:

ONE SAID: It's dark in here, isn't it?
THE OTHER REPLIED: I don't know; I can't see.

Why are blond jokes so short?
So men can remember them.

The superiority theory is one of the main accounts of humour, with ancient roots and long-standing acceptance. However, this account has several weaknesses and limitations. I do not intend to expand on this point here and will only outline certain basic problems faced by this theory.[10]

First, there is the evident problem that there exist non-humorous manifestations of superiority. Insults constitute a clear example of such: speakers can use insults to ridicule the addressee and show their own superiority, but insults are not typically funny. On a different level, we can feel superior to many things without feeling any joy or amusement in it: we can feel superior to infants, to pets or to less developed countries without in any way feeling the urge to laugh at them. Curcó illustrates this point with a crushing example: 'Abused slaves must often have felt sudden bursts of moral superiority over plantation owners, which presumably had little to do with experiencing humor' (Curcó 1997: 19).

Thus, not every feeling of superiority amuses or is perceived as funny and humorous. This could still lead to a weak version of the superiority theory: humour is generated by feelings of superiority, but not every feeling of superiority generates humour.

---

[8] Morreall (1987); Scruton (1987); Gruner (1997).
[9] I collected the following jokes from the Laughtfactory website: www .laughfactory.com/.
[10] For a clear elaboration of this issue, see, for instance, Curcó (1997).

140   7 SARCASM AND HUMOUR

However, an immediate limitation suggests just the opposite: not every humorous instance is produced by a feeling of superiority; that is, not all humour must be derisive. Clear examples of this type are common and well-known absurdist or knock-knock jokes such as the following:

> How does an elephant hide in a strawberry patch? It paints its toenails red. (Ritchie 2013: 128)
>
> Q: What did the square say to the circle?
> A: Haven't I seen you around?
>
> Q: What did the square say to the cube?
> A: You have put on weight lately!
>
> Knock Knock.
> Who's there?
> Tank!
> Tank who?
> You're welcome.[11]

These types of jokes are not typically based on a feeling of superiority, and they can still be considered funny. This would further limit the superiority theory of humour: humour may sometimes be generated by feelings of superiority, but not every feeling of superiority generates humour, nor does all humour originate from a feeling of superiority.

Nevertheless, this weaker version of the theory can help us shed light on what presently concerns us. If feelings of superiority can sometimes create a humorous feeling, it may well explain why at least certain instances of irony are considered funny. Let us not forget that one of the central features of irony is that the speaker always expresses an attitude that is typically negative. In irony, then, the speaker tends to criticize, mock, tease, ridicule or make fun of someone or something. It appears correct to state that in irony, then, the speaker tends to express a feeling of superiority towards the target of her irony. This could thus be an explanation for the link between humour and irony in terms of the superiority view: irony is often funny because irony often expresses a negative attitude that places the speaker in a superior position, and it is this feeling of superiority that creates the humour. This is the case in the following examples, in which the speaker manifests superiority with regard to the target of her criticism, resulting in a humorous ironic remark:

---

[11] Source: www.jokes4us.com.

7.2 Irony and Humour

s u e (pointing to Jack, who has become a total nuisance after drinking some wine):

(16) As they say, a glass of wine is good for you!

> (Wilson & Sperber 2012: 130)

Suppose that Bill, who wants everybody to think of him as a totally sincere person, tells a transparent lie and believes that he is believed. Judy says ironically:

(26) What a clever lie!

> (Sperber 1984: 33)

(35) How about another small slice of pizza?

> to someone who has just gobbled up the whole pie.

> (Kumon-Nakamura et al. 1995: 4)

Activity 7.2.1 Humour, Irony and Superiority

Think about a couple of jokes that made you laugh.

1. Is there any expression of superiority in them?
   Now recall the samples of irony you used in previous chapters.
2. Would you say that they are funny?
3. Is there an obvious or remarkable expression of superiority in them? If so, would you say that it makes the examples funny?

7.2.2 Incongruity Theories of Humour

While the superiority theory of irony may be the most ancient one, 'incongruity theories' are probably the most acclaimed and accepted by current theorists.[12] Incongruity theories have an antique origin as well – Aristotle mentioned in his *Rhetoric* that if you want to make your audience laugh, you should set expectations and then fail to fulfil them. However, it was long after Aristotle's work that the incongruity theories of humour and laughter developed into more elaborate accounts.

---

[12] See Yus (2017) for an up-to-date study of the incongruity-resolution model in pragmatic terms.

142 7 SARCASM AND HUMOUR

In the eighteenth and nineteenth centuries, certain philosophers signalled the importance of incongruity resolution (as we would call it today) to create humour. Immanuel Kant explained that laughter arises when an expectation is suddenly transformed into nothing (Kant, *Critique of Judgment*: 1, 1, 54), and Arthur Schopenhauer suggested that it is when a concept and the real objects that have been thought through it are incongruent that we laugh, because humour arises (Schopenhauer 1818: 1, 13). Søren Kierkegaard[13] also viewed humour as the product of a discrepancy between what may be expected and what actually occurs (Kierkegaard 1846).

The idea that an incongruity results in a humorous response has been elaborated into different theories, particularly since the last decades of the twentieth century. Without entering into much detail, the general idea of incongruity theories of humour is that humour arises when we perceive an incongruity as something is expected and the expectation fails to materialize. As Curcó states,

> The basic idea underlying incongruity theories is also a simple one. We have come to expect certain patterns, properties and events in what we experience as a fairly orderly world. When something does not fit those patterns, we laugh. (Curcó 1997: 29)

Incongruity theories have typically been criticized for being overly general. Indeed, it is not easy to delimitate when two things are in fact incongruent: is it when they do not match each other, or when they contradict one another, or when they fall into a particular way of being different? Furthermore, it is obvious that not every incongruity is funny or gives rise to humour: things that we absolutely do not expect may occur that make us feel surprised, angry, scared or disgusted. Thus, it should be explained why some incongruities are humorous and others are not.

Overall, the general idea of incongruity appears to be relatively helpful to explain common humorous instances, such as stand-up comedy or ambiguity-based jokes[14]:

> I SAID TO THE GYM INSTRUCTOR: Can you teach me to do the splits?
> HE SAID: How flexible are you?
> I SAID: I can't make Tuesdays.

---

[13] Who, indeed, wrote his doctoral thesis on irony (Kierkegaard 1841).

[14] I collected a number of the following jokes from the LaughLab website: www.richardwiseman.com/LaughLab/home.html.

7.2 Irony and Humour 143

Two hunters are out in the woods when one of them collapses. He does not seem to be breathing and his eyes are glazed. The other guy whips out his phone and calls the emergency services.

HE GASPS: My friend is dead! What can I do?
THE OPERATOR SAYS: Calm down. I can help. First, let's make sure he's dead.

(There is a silence, and then a shot is heard.)

BACK ON THE PHONE, THE GUY SAYS: OK, now what?

A patient says: 'Doctor, last night I made a Freudian slip. I was having dinner with my mother-in-law and wanted to say, "Could you please pass the butter". However, instead I said, "You silly cow, you have completely ruined my life"'.

EMPLOYEE: Boss, I love your new car.
BOSS: Thank you! If you work hard and you do some overtime, I will be able to buy an even bigger one.

As with the superiority theories, it thus appears that a general idea of incongruity may be present in certain humorous instances. This weak version of the theory is sufficient for us at present because what we really want to do is determine how the idea of incongruity can relate to irony and shed light on the typical presence of humour in ironic communication.

In the early chapters of this book, we observed that there are different ways in which ironic utterances are explained within pragmatics. However, there are two points that most theories share: the ironic speaker expresses a typically negative attitude (which is similar to the way humour is produced according to the superiority theories), and she does not properly *say* or *assert* the literal meaning of her utterance. Instead, different theories claim that the speaker echoes a proposition, pretends or implicates something different (or even contradictory). Overall, it appears correct to say that every theory accepts that there is some type of clash in irony: the speaker does not intend to *say* what she puts forward but something different (or an attitude towards what she does not say).

This clash at the heart of ironic communication can explain why ironic examples are typically considered to be humorous. It is incongruous – in the broad and general sense of incongruity we are working with – for the speaker to put forward content that she does not intend to communicate, particularly when she shows this lack of

144　　　　　　　　　　　　　　　　　7 SARCASM AND HUMOUR

commitment overtly, instead of hiding it. The incongruity is resolved as soon as the hearer realizes that the speaker has not truthfully *said* this meaning but instead has put it forward to make the hearer understand what she truly wants to communicate. Thus, in line with the incongruity theories, we can expect that resolving the incongruity may create humour for the hearer as a side effect; that is, the hearer may find the speaker's utterance humorous. This may be why the following examples of irony, in which the incongruity between what the speaker is putting forward and what she actually intends to communicate is relatively evident, show a sense of humour:

(28)　Outside temperature is again below freezing point: a true heat wave!

　　　(Sperber 1984: 33)

(47)　Heard about your latest anti-proton decay experiment. 20,000 data runs and no statistically significant results. Very impressive.

Activity 7.2.2 Humour, Irony and Incongruity
Turn again to the jokes you remembered for the preceding activity. 　1.　Do they involve any incongruity resolution? 　　　Now revisit the examples of irony you used in the previous chapters. 　2.　Is there a manifest incongruity resolution involved? If so, would you say that it makes the examples funny?

7.2.3 Summary

In this section, I attempted to shed light on a claim that is typically accepted or taken for granted both among natural speakers and on the theoretical level: irony has some type of relationship with humour, or, if you prefer, irony is often funny. This general claim can be explained if we look at the main theories of linguistic humour. According to the superiority theory of humour, humour arises when a feeling of superiority is expressed. As ironic speakers typically express attitudes of mockery, criticism, blame and so on, it is easy to understand in terms of superiority that certain instances of irony are funny. Alternatively, according to the incongruity theory of humour, humour arises when some type of incongruity is resolved – when something was expected but then failed to occur. This view of the issue can also help us to

7.3 Suggested Reading 145

explain the links between irony and humour: as a shift in meaning is typically present in irony, it could explain why certain ironic instances are humorous in terms of incongruity.

Thus, it is understandable that irony and humour are viewed as related because irony has certain basic elements that make it a good candidate for producing a humorous effect. The readings in the following list can help to further develop these ideas.

7.3 SUGGESTED READING

7.3.1 Sarcasm

The following works elaborate on the notion of sarcasm and its relationship with irony:

Dynel, M. 2016. Pejoration via sarcastic irony and sarcasm. In *Pejoration*, ed. R. Finkbeiner, J. Meibauer and H. Wiese, 219–40. Amsterdam: John Benjamins.

McDonald, S. 2000. Neuropsychological studies of sarcasm. *Metaphor and Symbol* 15(1–2): 85–98.

Rockwell, P. 2000. Lower, slower, louder: vocal cues of sarcasm. *Journal of Psycholinguistic Research* 29(5): 483–95.

7.3.2 Humour

There are a number of works on humour from a linguistic standpoint. Here are several that will be helpful for a general view of the issue:

Attardo, S. 1994. *Linguistic Theories of Humor*. Berlin: Mouton de Gruyter.

Curcó, C. 1997. The pragmatics of humorous interpretations: a relevance-theoretic approach. PhD dissertation, University College London.

Goatly, A. 2012. *Meaning and Humor* (Key Topics in Semantics and Pragmatics). New York: Cambridge University Press.

Monreall, J. (ed.). 1987. *The Philosophy of Laughter and Humor*. Albany: State University of New York Press.

Yus, F. 2016. *Humor and Relevance*. Philadelphia: John Benjamins.

The following papers focus on the relationship between irony and humour:

Attardo, S. 2001. Humor and irony in interaction: from mode adoption to failure of detection. In *Say Not to Say: New Perspectives on Miscommunication*, ed. L. Anolli, R. Ciceri & G. Riva, 165–85. Amsterdam: IOS Press.

Dynel, M. 2013b. When does irony tickle the hearer? Towards capturing the characteristics of humorous irony. In *Developments in Linguistic Humor Theory*, ed. Marta Dynel, 289–320. Amsterdam: John Benjamins.

Garmendia, J. 2014. The clash: humor and critical attitude in verbal irony. *Humor* 27(4): 641–59.

Examples Used in Text

> Maia and Ku are good friends and know each other well. Ku always raves about women driving terribly, and Maia always argues with him on this, saying that it is nonsense to correlate one's gender with one's driving ability. Today, they both see someone crashing a car with a traffic light foolishly. When they approach the car, they both see that the driver is a man. Maia claims:
>
> (0)   That was a clumsy woman driving.

Ku (who always says that women are terrible drivers) sees a woman elegantly manoeuvring a car into a small and tricky parking spot. Then it is Ku himself who claims:

> (0')   That was a clumsy woman driving.

> (1)   He is an Englishman; he is, therefore, brave. (Grice 1967a/89: 25)

> (2)   X is meeting a woman this evening. (Grice 1967a/89: 37)

> X, with whom A has been on close terms until now, has betrayed a secret of A's to a business rival. A and his audience both know this. A says:
>
> (3)   X is a fine friend. (Grice 1967a/89: 34)

A and B are walking down the street, and they both see a car with a shattered window. B says:

> (4)   Look, that car has all its windows intact. (Grice 1967b/89: 53)

148   *Examples Used in Text*

During the precept, Danny was dominating the discussion. He certainly seemed to be familiar with the subject, but he was obnoxious in the way he showed off his knowledge. Jesse, one of Danny's classmates, said:

(5)   You sure know a lot. (Kumon-Namakura et al. 1995: 7)

Bill is a neurotically cautious driver who keeps his petrol tank full, never fails to indicate when turning and repeatedly scans the horizon for possible dangers. His companion says:

(6)   I really appreciate cautious drivers. (Wilson 2006: 1726)

A mother says to her teenage son:

(7)   I love children who keep their rooms clean,

just as she has discovered that her son, once again, failed to clean his room. (Gibbs & O'Brien 1991: 525)

Bill is a neurotically cautious driver who keeps his petrol tank full, never fails to indicate when turning and repeatedly scans the horizon for possible dangers. His companion says:

(8)   Don't forget to use your indicator.

(9)   Do you think we should stop for petrol? (Wilson 2006: 1726)

MARY: What shall we do today?
PETER: (10) It is a lovely day for a picnic.

JANE: Do you have plans for today?
MARY: (11) It is a lovely day for a picnic, Peter thinks.

MARY: What shall we do today?
PETER: (10) It is a lovely day for a picnic.
MARY: (12) It is a lovely day for a picnic! Yay! It is too long we have
            not been at the valley!
            (13) It is a lovely day for a picnic, did you check the weather
            forecast?
            (14) It is a lovely day for a picnic. It is *always* a lovely day for
            a picnic for you.

Examples Used in Text 149

PETER: It's a lovely day for a picnic.
They go for a picnic and it rains.
MARY (sarcastically):

(15) It's a lovely day for a picnic, indeed. (Sperber & Wilson 1986/
95: 239)

SUE (pointing to Jack, who has become a total nuisance after
drinking some wine):

(16) As they say, a glass of wine is good for you! (Wilson & Sperber
2012: 130)

Nancy and her friend Jane were planning a trip to the beach.
'It's probably going to rain tomorrow', said Jane, who worked for
a local TV station as a meteorologist.
The next day was a warm and sunny one.
As she looked out of the window, Nancy said:

(17) This certainly is awful weather.

Nancy and her friend Jane were planning a trip to the beach.
'The weather should be nice tomorrow', said Jane, who worked
for a local TV station as a meteorologist.
The next day was a cold and stormy one.
As she looked out of the window, Nancy said:

(18) This certainly is beautiful weather. (Wilson & Sperber 2012: 128)

MARY (after a boring party):

(19) That was fun. (Wilson & Sperber 2012: 123)

Mary and someone she does not know are waiting for an elevator
after having left a funeral. It has been long and boring – as funerals
are expected to be in their shared culture. Mary says:

(20) That was fun!

We walk in a rather posh neighbourhood and come upon gorgeous
Ferraris and Jaguars. I say:

(21) What a junkyard! (Giora 1998: 2)

150   *Examples Used in Text*

(22)   Would you very much mind if I asked you, please, to perhaps consider cleaning up your room sometime this month? (Kreuz & Glucksberg 1989: 383)

Said on a very rainy day:

(23)   I think the washing hasn't dried. (Giora 1995: 246)

'Do you know any G.M.?', my friend asks.

(24)   'Rings a bell',

I reply (given that the person in question is well known to the speakers). (Giora 1995: 246)

DINA: I missed the last news broadcast. What did the Prime Minister say about the Palestinians?
MIRA (with ridiculing aversion):

(25)   That we should deport them. (Giora 1995: 246)

Suppose Bill, who wants everybody to think of him as a totally sincere person, tells a transparent lie and believes he is believed. Judy says ironically:

(26)   What a clever lie! (Sperber 1984: 33)

(27)   Jones, this murderer, this thief, this crook, is indeed an honourable fellow! (Sperber 1984: 33)

(28)   Outside temperature is again below freezing point: a true heat wave! (Sperber 1984: 33)

(29)   What lovely weather! (Sperber 1984: 134)

Against Judy's advice, Bill bought what a crooked art dealer told him was a true Picasso. Roger, claiming to be competent, vouched for the painting's authenticity. Other friends of Bill's were much impressed by the painting until a genuine expert at last showed it to be a fake. When Judy then says:

(30)   That was a truly beautiful Picasso! (Sperber 1984: 134)

Examples Used in Text 151

Imagine that Bill is prone to say of himself: 'I am a very patient person'. In response to a display of temper from Bill, Judy says, ironically:

(31) Bill is such a patient person. (Currie 2006: 119)

Consider a situation in which two people approach a door. The first person to reach the door opens it and lets it swing shut behind her. The second person, carrying a heavy box, says:

(32) Don't hold the door open. I'll just say 'open sesame'

or

(33) Thanks for holding the door. (Kumon-Nakamura et al. 1995: 4)

(34) How old did you say you were?

said to someone acting inappropriately for his or her age. (Kumon-Nakamura et al. 1995: 4)

(35) How about another small slice of pizza?

to someone who has just gobbled up the whole pie. (Kumon-Nakamura et al. 1995: 4)

(36) Would you mind very much if I asked you to consider cleaning up your room sometime this year?

to an inconsiderate and slovenly housemate. (Kumon-Nakamura et al. 1995: 4–5)

Nancy and her friend Jane were planning a trip to the beach. 'It's probably going to rain tomorrow', said Jane, who was always trying, with little success, to predict the weather. The next day was a warm and sunny one. As she looked out the window, Nancy said:

(37) This certainly is awful weather. (Kreuz & Glucksberg 1989: 377)

Suppose that I have a friend who is not very self-confident and after an examination he says: 'I'm going to fail this exam. I did it all wrong'. After some days I meet him and he tells me that

152　　　　　　　　　　　　　　　　　　　　*Examples Used in Text*

he has passed the exam with a very good mark. Then I could
ironically say:

> (38)　Oh yes, you have failed, you did it all wrong, you are a very
> bad student! (Alba-Juez 1995: 11)

Spoken by your stock broker on calling for the third time to
announce unexpected dividends:

> (39)　Sorry to keep bothering you like this. (Brown 1980: 114,
> quoted in Attardo 2000: 796)

An adult addressing a child:

> (40)　Oh, how small you have grown! (Haverkate 1990: 90)

In a conversation between two lovers:

> (41)　I don't like you at all! (Haverkate 1990: 90)

Claudio's stockbroker calls for the third time to announce unexpected dividends. Claudio answers quite rudely: 'You again? What
is it now?'. The broker replies:

> (42)　Sorry to keep bothering you like this. (Garmendia 2010: 411)

> (43)　Isn't it the loveliest day ever to go for a picnic?

> (44)　I have never seen such a nice and lovely day for a picnic.

> (45)　I am delighted that we can have a picnic just on the loveliest day
> ever.

Jaime and Lu go to Hawaii on their honeymoon. They had dreamed
about sunny weather and the beach. Unfortunately, the weather
was terrible during their stay. It did not stop raining, it was awfully
windy, and they even had a hurricane. The day they came back
home, Christina picks them up at the airport. They are pale, and
they look tired, frustrated and angry. Christina asks politely, 'So,
how was Hawaii?' Jaime replies dryly:

> (46)　Wonderful.

Examples Used in Text 153

(47) Heard about your latest anti-proton decay experiment. 20,000 data runs and no statistically significant results. Very impressive.

(48) Me? I like wearing a condom. It means I'm having sex. I already spend most of my time *not* wearing one. It's like a tuxedo – I enjoy putting one on for special occasions. (Mazzucchelli 2009: 57)

(49) America's allies – always there when they need you. (Kaufer 1981: 501)

(50) Both the Penguins and the Porpoises had the most powerful army in the world. (Zalecki 1990: 128; attributed by the author to Anatole France)

(51) Wait, I'm trying to imagine you with a personality.

Glossary

Assertive In speech act theory, assertive speech acts are those which commit the speaker to something being the case (other kinds within the classification of speech acts are directives, commissives, expressives and declaratives).

Bridge content According to the *asif*-theory, a speaker when being ironic communicates a bunch of implicatures. Among them there is one that is special because it is closely linked to the content that the speaker makes as if to say. This implicature is called the 'bridge content' of the utterance, as it is the bridge that leads the hearer to further implicatures in the ironic content.

Clue (or cue) A speaker when being ironic can use some strategies to facilitate the hearer's understanding of the irony. These clues include the speaker's tone of voice, stylistic choices and gestures. According to the *asif*-theory, they should also include opposition, echo and pretence.

Cooperative principle According to Grice, every speaker follows this principle – together with some conversational maxims (*see* Maxims) – when engaged in a conversation. It is by breaking these principle and maxims that speakers communicate implicatures.

Critical pragmatics A pragmatic account led by Kepa Korta and John Perry. The *asif*-theory is an application of this general theory to ironic communication.

Declarative Sentences are classified taking into account their role in the discourse. Within this classification, declarative sentences are those which are used to make statements or convey information.

Echoic In relevance theory, echoic utterances are those which convey the speaker's attitude towards a thought or utterance which the speaker attributes to someone other than herself at the current time.

Exploit (a maxim) According to Grice, a conversational maxim is exploited when the speaker flouts that maxim – that is, she blatantly fails to fulfil it (*see* Flout) – in order to communicate an implicature.

Face In politeness theory, 'face' (which can be positive or negative) is the public self-image that every person attempts to protect (from face-threatening acts).

Glossary 155

Flout (a maxim) In terms of Grice's theory of conversation, a speaker can fail to fulfil a conversational maxim in different ways. The speaker flouts a maxim when she *blatantly* fails to fulfil it.

Illocutionary act In terms of speech act theory, every speech act encompasses three levels: the speaker *says* something (locutionary act), by saying something the speaker *does* something (illocutionary act) and by so doing the speaker produces some *effects* on the audience (perlocutionary act).

Implicature According to Grice, a speaker communicates by an utterance more than what she says. Implicatures are generated by failing to fulfil (*see* Exploit, Flout) some conversational maxim. What one communicates is the sum of what she says and what she implicates. Implicatures are characterized by being indeterminate, and they have three central characteristics: they are calculable, cancellable and non-detachable. There are different kinds of implicatures: conventional, conversational, generalized and particularized.

Intonation The variation of vocal pitch used to convey grammatical information or the expression of attitudes or emotions.

Maxims According to Grice, there are some conversational maxims that govern human conversation together with the cooperative principle. He named the following maxims: quantity, quality, relation and manner.

Mention (versus Use) In relevance theory terms, when a speaker mentions an expression, she makes reference to the expression itself; when a speaker uses an expression, she makes reference to what the expression refers to. If the speaker mentions a whole sentence, the resulting utterance does not have the illocutionary force corresponding to a standard use of such a sentence. Irony was defined as a case of echoic mention in the first works of relevance theory.

Preparatory conditions Speech acts have some constitutive rules that explain how an illocutionary act is performed successfully. Among them, preparatory conditions explain what the speaker implies in performing certain illocutionary acts. Other conditions include propositional content, sincerity and essential rules.

Principles of relevance Relevance theory formulates two main principles of relevance: 1. *First (cognitive) principle of relevance:* Human cognition is geared towards the maximization of relevance (that is, to the achievement of as many contextual (cognitive) effects as possible for as little processing effort as possible). 2. *Second (communicative) principle of relevance:* Every act of ostensive communication (for example, an utterance) communicates a presumption of its own optimal relevance.

Relevance theory A pragmatic theory presented by Deirdre Wilson and Dan Sperber. It is an inferential model of communication as it considers intention recognition to be central in human communication. As Grice, they claim that utterances create expectations of relevance that guide the hearer, and they develop a general theory of communication based on that idea (*see* Principles of relevance).

156   *Glossary*

Salience A meaning of a word or an expression is salient if it is coded in the mental lexicon. There can be different degrees of salience, affected by factors such as conventionality, frequency, familiarity and prototypicality. The graded salience hypothesis attempts to explain ironic communication in terms of salience.

Sincerity conditions Speech acts have some constitutive rules that explain how an illocutionary act is performed successfully. Among them, sincerity conditions explain what psychological state the speaker expresses to be in. Other conditions include propositional content, preparatory and essential rules.

Speech act theory A theory of language propounded by Austin based primarily on the consideration of language as action – or how people by using language not only can *say* things but also can *do* things. Searle was one of the first developers of the theory, and he formulated the constitutive rules of speech acts (*see* Sincerity conditions, Preparatory conditions).

Strong/weak implicature In terms of relevance theory, an implicature is strongly communicated when the intention to communicate this implicature is made highly mutually manifest. The strength of an implicature is a matter of degree and varies from highly strong implicatures to clearly weak implicatures (for example, implicatures in evocative metaphor).

Target *See* Victim

Use (versus Mention) *See* Mention

Utterance An utterance is the act of uttering a sentence in a certain time and place. The term is also used to name the product of this action. Utterances include written, signed or spoken tokens – but the latter are the most commonly considered ones in pragmatics. They are specific events, so the same sentence uttered by another speaker, at another time or in a different place would constitute a different utterance.

Victim Speakers when being ironic always express an attitude. The target of this attitude is called the victim (or butt) of the irony.

Bibliography

Alba-Juez, L. 1995. Irony and politeness. *Revista Española de Lingüística Aplicada* 10: 9–16.

Alba-Juez, L. & S. Attardo. 2014. The evaluative palette of verbal irony. In *Evaluation in Context*, ed. G. Thompson & L. Alba-Juez, 93–115. Amsterdam: John Benjamins.

Amante, D. J. 1981. The theory of ironic speech acts. *Poetics Today* 2(2): 77–96.

Aristotle. 1984. *Rhetoric*. In *The Rhetoric and the Poetics of Aristotle*, trans. R. Roberts & I. Bywater. New York: Modern Library.

Attardo, S. 1994. *Linguistic Theories of Humor*. Berlin: de Gruyter.

2000. Irony as relevant inappropriateness. *Journal of Pragmatics* 32: 793–826.

2001. Humor and irony in interaction: from mode adoption to failure of detection. In *Say Not to Say: New Perspectives on Miscommunication*, ed. L. Anolli, R. Ciceri & G. Riva, 165–85. Amsterdam: IOS Press.

Attardo, S., J. Eisterhold, J. Hay & I. Poggi. 2003. Multimodal markers of irony and sarcasm. *Humor* 16(2): 243–60.

Attardo, S., L. Pickering & A. Baker. 2011. Prosodic and multimodal markers of humor in conversation. *Pragmatics & Cognition* 19(2): 224–47.

Austin, J. L. 1962. *How to Do Things with Words*. Oxford: Oxford University Press.

Bach, K. 1999. The myth of conventional implicature. *Linguistics and Philosophy* 22: 327–66.

Barbe, K. 1995. *Irony in Context*. Amsterdam: John Benjamins.

Booth, W. 1974. *A Rhetoric of Irony*. Chicago: University of Chicago Press.

Boucher, J. & C. E. Osgood. 1969. The Pollyanna hypothesis. *Journal of Verbal Learning and Verbal Behavior* 8: 1–8.

Brown, P. & S. C. Levinson. 1987. *Politeness: Some Universals in Language Use*. New York: Cambridge University Press.

Brown, R. L., Jr. 1980. The pragmatics of verbal irony. In *Language Use and the Uses of Language*, ed. R. W. Shuy & A. Shnukal, 111–27. Washington, DC: Georgetown University Press.

Bryant, G. A. & J. E. Fox Tree. 2005. Is there an ironic tone of voice? *Language and Speech* 48(3): 257–77.

158 *Bibliography*

Camp, E. 2012. Sarcasm, pretense, and the semantics/pragmatics distinction. *Noûs* 46(4): 587–634.

Carroll, N. 2013. Expression, music and dance. In *Thinking Through Dance: The Philosophy of Dance Performance and Practices*, ed. J. Bunker, A. Pakes & B. Rowell, 150–64. Hampshire: Dance Books.

Carston, R. 2002. *Thoughts and Utterances*. Oxford: Blackwell.

Carston, R. & C. Wearing. 2015. Hyperbolic language and its relation to metaphor and irony. *Journal of Pragmatics* 79: 79–92.

Chevallier, C., I. Noveck, F. Happé & D. Wilson. 2011. What's in a voice? Prosody as a test case for the theory of mind account of autism. *Neuropsychologia* 49: 507–17.

Clark, H. H. & R. J. Gerrig. 1984. On the pretense theory of irony. *Journal of Experimental Psychology: General* 113(1): 121–26.

Colston, H. L. 1997. Salting a wound or sugaring a pill: the pragmatic functions of ironic criticism. *Discourse Processes* 23: 25–45.

Colston, H. L. & R. W. Gibbs. 2002. Are irony and metaphor understood differently? *Metaphor and Symbol* 17(1): 57–80.

Colston, H. L. & J. O'Brien. 2000. Contrast and pragmatics in figurative language: anything understatement can do, irony can do better. *Journal of Pragmatics* 32: 1557–83.

Curcó, C. 1997. The pragmatics of humorous interpretations: a relevance-theoretic approach. PhD dissertation, University College London.

2000. Irony: negation, echo and metarepresentation. *Lingua* 110: 257–80.

Currie, G. 2006. Why irony is pretence. In *The Architecture of the Imagination*, ed. S. Nichols, 111–33. Oxford: Oxford University Press.

Dews, S. & E. Winner. 1995. Muting the meaning: a social function of irony. *Metaphor and Symbolic Activity* 10: 3–19.

1999. Obligatory processing of literal and nonliteral meanings in verbal irony. *Journal of Pragmatics* 31: 1579–99.

Dews, S., J. Kaplan & E. Winner. 1995. Why not say it directly? The social functions of irony. *Discourse Processes* 19: 347–67.

Dufour, N., E. Redcay, L. Young, et al. 2013. Similar brain activation during false belief tasks in a large sample of adults with and without autism. *PLoS ONE* 8(9): e75468.

Dynel, M. 2013a. Irony from a neo-Gricean perspective: on untruthfulness and evaluative implicature. *Intercultural Pragmatics* 10(3): 403–31.

2013b. When does irony tickle the hearer? Towards capturing the characteristics of humorous irony. In *Developments in Linguistic Humour Theory*, ed. M. Dynel, 289–320. Amsterdam: John Benjamins.

2016. Pejoration via sarcastic irony and sarcasm. In *Pejoration*, ed. R. Finkbeiner, J. Meibauer & H. Wiese, 219–40. Amsterdam: John Benjamins.

Elleström, L. 1996. Some notes on irony in the visual arts and music: the examples of Magritte and Shostakovich. *Word & Image: A Journal of Verbal/Visual Enquiry* 12(2): 197–208.

Bibliography

Filik, R., E. Brightman, C. Gathercole & H. Leuthold. 2017. The emotional impact of verbal irony: eye-tracking evidence for a two-stage process. *Journal of Memory and Language* 93: 193–202.

Fowler, H. W. 1965. *A Dictionary of Modem English Usage* (2nd edn). Oxford: Oxford University Press.

Garmendia, J. 2010. Irony is critical. *Pragmatics and Cognition* 18(2): 397–421.

2011. She's (not) a fine friend: 'saying' and criticism in irony. *Intercultural Pragmatics* 8(1): 41–65.

2013. Ironically saying and implicating. In *What Is Said and What Is Not: The Semantics/Pragmatics Interface*, ed. C. Penco & F. Domaneschi, 225–41. Stanford: CSLI Publications.

2014. The clash: humour and critical attitude in verbal irony. *International Journal of Humor Research* 27(4): 641–59.

2015. A (neo-)Gricean account of irony: an answer to relevance theory. *International Review of Pragmatics* 7: 40–79.

Garmendia, J. & K. Korta. 2007. The point of irony. In *Language, Representation and Reasoning*, ed. M. Aurnague, K. Korta & J.M. Larrazabal, 189–200. Bilbao: UPV-EHU.

Gibbs, R. W. & H. L. Colston. 2001. The risks and rewards of ironic communication. In *Say Not to Say: New Perspectives on Miscommunication*, ed. L. Anolli, R. Ciceri & G. Riva, 187–200. Amsterdam: IOS Press.

Gibbs, R. W. & H. L. Colston (eds.). 2007. *Irony in Language and Thought: A Cognitive Science Reader*. New York: Erlbaum Associates.

Gibbs, R. W. & J. O'Brien. 1991. Psychological aspects of irony understanding. *Journal of Pragmatics* 16: 523–30.

Giora, R. 1995. On irony and negation. *Discourse Processes* 19: 239–64.

1998. Irony. In *Handbook of Pragmatics*, ed. J. Verschueren, J. Ostman, J. Blommaert & C. Bulcaen. Amsterdam: John Benjamins.

Giora, R., O. Fein & T. Schwartz. 1998. Irony: graded salience and indirect negation. *Metaphor and Symbol* 13(2): 83–101.

Goatly, A. 2012. *Meaning and Humor: Key Topics in Semantics and Pragmatics*. New York: Cambridge University Press.

Grice, H. P. 1967a/89. Logic and conversation. In *The Logic of Grammar*, ed. D. Davidson & G. Harman, 1975, 64–75. Encino: Dickenson. Also in *Syntax and Semantics 3: Speech Acts*, ed. P. Cole & J. L. Morgan, 1975, 41–58. New York: Academic Press. Reprinted in H. P. Grice (1989), 22–40.

1967b/89. Further notes on logic and conversation. In *Syntax and Semantics 9: Pragmatics*, ed. P. Cole, 1978, 113–127. New York: Academic Press. Reprinted in H. P. Grice (1989), 41–57.

1981/89. Presupposition and conversational implicature. In *Radical Pragmatics*, ed. P. Cole, 1981, 183–97. New York: Academic Press. Reprinted in H. P. Grice (1989), 269–82.

1989. *Studies in the Way of Words*. Cambridge, MA: Harvard University Press.

160   *Bibliography*

Gruner, C. R. 1997. *The Game of Humor: A Comprehensive Theory of Why We Laugh*. New Brunswick, NJ: Transaction Publishers.

Haiman, J. 1998. *Talk Is Cheap: Sarcasm, Alienation, and the Evolution of Language*. New York: Oxford University Press.

Hamamoto, H. 1998. Irony from a cognitive perspective. In *Relevance Theory: Applications and Implications*, ed. R. Carston & S. Uchida, 257–70. Amsterdam: John Benjamins.

Happé, F. 1993. Communicative competence and theory of mind in autism: A test of relevance theory. *Cognition* 48: 101–119.

Haverkate, H. 1990. A speech act analysis of irony. *Journal of Pragmatics* 14 (1): 77–109.

Hirsch, G. 2010. Explicitations and other types of shifts in the translation of irony and humor. *Target* 23(2): 178–205.

Horn, L. R. & G. Ward (eds.). 2004. *The Handbook of Pragmatics*. Oxford: Blackwell.

Jorgensen, J. 1996. The functions of sarcastic irony in speech. *Journal of Pragmatics* 26: 613–634.

Jorgensen, J., G. A. Miller & D. Sperber. 1984. Test of the mention theory of irony. *Journal of Experimental Psychology: General* 113(1): 112–120.

Kant, I. 1892. *Critique of Judgement*. (In *Kant's Critique of Judgement*, trans. with Introduction and Notes by J. H. Bernard (2nd edn revised), 1914. London: Macmillan.)

Karttunen, L. & S. Peters. 1979. Conventional implicature. In *Syntax and Semantics 11: Presupposition*, ed. C. K. Oh & D. A. Dinneen, 1–56. New York: Academic Press.

Kaufer, D. 1981. Understanding ironic communication. *Journal of Pragmatics* 5: 495–510.

Kierkegaard, S. 1841. *On the Concept of Irony with Continual Reference to Socrates*, ed. H. V. Hong & E. H. Hong, 1992. Princeton, NJ: Princeton University Press.

1846. *Concluding Unscientific Postscript*, trans. D. Swenson & W. Lowrie, 1941. Princeton, NJ: Princeton University Press.

Korta, K. & J. Perry. 2006. Pragmatics. In *The Stanford Encyclopedia of Philosophy* (Winter 2006 edn), ed. E. N. Zalta. Available at http://plato.stanford.edu/archives/spr2007/entries/pragmatics/.

2007a. Radical minimalism, moderate contextualism. In *Context-Sensitivity and Semantic Minimalism: Essays on Semantics and Pragmatics*, ed. G. Preyer & G. Peter, 94–111. Oxford: Oxford University Press.

2007b. How to say things with words. In *John Searle's Philosophy of Language: Force, Meaning, and Thought*, ed. S. L. Tsohatzidis, 169–189. Cambridge: Cambridge University Press.

2011. *Critical Pragmatics: An Inquiry into Reference and Communication*. Cambridge: Cambridge University Press.

Bibliography

Kreuz, R. J. & S. Glucksberg. 1989. How to be sarcastic: the echoic reminder theory of verbal irony. *Journal of Experimental Psychology: General* 118(4): 374–86.

Kreuz, R. J. & R. M. Roberts. 1995. Two cues for verbal irony: hyperbole and the ironic tone of voice. *Metaphor and Symbolic Activity* 10(1): 21–31.

Kreuz, R. J., D. Long & M. Church. 1991. On being ironic: pragmatic and mnemonic implications. *Metaphor and Symbolic Activity* 6(3): 149–62.

Kumon-Nakamura, S., S. Glucksberg & M. Brown. 1995. How about another piece of pie: the allusional pretense theory of discourse irony. *Journal of Experimental Psychology: General* 124(1): 3–21.

Langdon, R., M. Coltheart, P. B. Ward & S. V. Catts. 2002. Disturbed communication in schizophrenia: the role of poor pragmatics and poor mind-reading. *Psychological Medicine* 32: 1273–84.

Levinson, S. 1983. *Pragmatics.* New York: Cambridge University Press.

Lucariello, J. 1994. Situational irony: a concept of events gone awry. *Journal of Experimental Psychology. General* 123(2): 129–45.

Matthews, J. K., J. T. Hancock & P. J. Dunham. 2006. The roles of politeness and humor in the asymmetry of affect in verbal irony. *Discourse Processes* 41(1): 3–24.

Mazzucchelli, D. 2009. *Asterios Polyp.* New York: Pantheon Books.

McDonald, S. 1999. Exploring the process of inference generation in sarcasm: a review of normal and clinical studies. *Brain & Language* 68: 486–506.

  2000. Neuropsychological studies of sarcasm. *Metaphor and Symbol* 15(1–2): 85–98.

Morreall, J. (ed.). 1987. *The Philosophy of Laughter and Humor.* Albany: State University of New York Press.

Muecke, D. 1969. *The Compass of Irony.* London: Methuen.

  1978. Irony markers. *Poetics* 7: 363–75.

Nunberg, G. 2001. *The Way We Talk Now: Commentaries on Language and Culture.* Boston: Houghton Mifflin.

Oxford Dictionary of English (3rd edn). 2010. Oxford: Oxford University Press.

Partington, A. 2007. Irony and reversal of evaluation. *Journal of Pragmatics* 39: 1547–69.

Perelman, C. & L. Olbrechts-Tyteca. 1971. *The New Rhetoric: A Treatise on Argumentation.* Notre Dame, IN: University of Notre Dame Press.

Quintilian. *Institutio Oratoria,* trans. H. E. Butler, 1921, Cambridge, MA: Harvard University Press.

Recanati, F. 2004. *Literal Meaning.* Cambridge: Cambridge University Press.

  2007. Indexicality, context and pretence. In *Pragmatics,* ed. N. Burton-Roberts, 213–29. Basingstoke: Palgrave Macmillan.

Reimer, M. 2013. Grice on irony and metaphor: discredited by the experimental evidence? *International Review of Pragmatics* 5: 1–33.

Ritchie, D. 2013. *Metaphor* (Key Topics in Semantics and Pragmatics). Cambridge: Cambridge University Press.

162 *Bibliography*

Roberts, R. M. & R. J. Kreuz. 1994. Why do people use figurative language? *Psychological Science* 5(3): 159–63.

Rockwell, P. 2000. Lower, slower, louder: vocal cues of sarcasm. *Journal of Psycholinguistic Research* 29(5): 483–95.

Rodríguez-Rosique, S. 2013. The power of inversion: irony, from utterance to discourse. In *Irony and Humour: From Pragmatics to Discourse*, ed. L. Ruiz-Gurillo & M. B. Alvarado-Ortega, 17–38. Amsterdam: John Benjamins.

Ryle, G. 1950. 'If', 'so', and 'because'. In *Philosophical Analysis*, ed. M. Black, 323–40. Ithaca, NY: Cornell University Press.

Schopenhauer, A. 1818. *The World as Will and Representation*, trans. E. F. J. Payne, 1958. New York: Dover Publications.

Scruton, R. 1987. Laughter. In *The Philosophy of Laughter and Humor*, ed. J. Morreall, 156–71. Albany: State University of New York Press.

Searle, J. 1969. *Speech Acts*. Cambridge: Cambridge University Press.

Seto, K. 1998. On non-echoic irony. In *Relevance Theory: Applications and Implications*, ed. R. Carston & S. Uchida, 239–55. Amsterdam: John Benjamins.

Sloane, T. O. (ed.). 2001. *Encyclopedia of Rhetoric*. Oxford: Oxford University Press.

Sperber, D. 1984. Verbal irony: pretense or echoic mention? *Journal of Experimental Psychology: General* 113(1): 130–436.

Sperber, D. & D. Wilson. 1981. Irony and the use-mention distinction. In *Radical Pragmatics*, ed. P. Cole, 295–318. New York: Academic Press.

1986/95. *Relevance. Communication and Cognition*. Oxford: Blackwell.

1998. Irony and relevance: a reply to Seto, Hamamoto and Yamanashi. In *Relevance Theory: Applications and Implications*, ed. R. Carston & S. Uchida, 283–93. Amsterdam: John Benjamins.

Spotorno, N., A. Cheylus, J-B. Van Der Henst & I. A. Noveck. 2013. What's behind a P600? Integration operations during irony processing. *PLoS ONE* 8(6): e66839.

Spotorno, N., E. Koun, J. Prado, J-B. Van Der Henst & I. A. Noveck. 2012. Neural evidence that utterance-processing entails mentalizing: the case of irony. *NeuroImage* 63: 25–39.

Toplak, M. & A. N. Katz. 2000. On the uses of sarcastic irony. *Journal of Pragmatics* 32: 1467–88.

Walton, K. 1990. *Mimesis as Make-Believe: On the Foundations of the Representational Arts*. Cambridge, MA: Harvard University Press.

2017. Meiosis, hyperbole, irony. *Philosophical Studies* 174(1): 105–20.

Wang, A. T., S. S. Lee, M. Sigman & M. Dapretto. 2006. Neural basis of irony comprehension in children with autism: the role of prosody and context. *Brain* 129(4): 932–43.

Wilson, D. 2006. The pragmatics of verbal irony: echo or pretence? *Lingua* 116: 1722–43.

Bibliography

2009. Irony and meta-representation. *UCL Working Papers in Linguistics* 21: 183–226.

2013. Irony comprehension: A developmental perspective. *Journal of Pragmatics* 59: 40–56.

Wilson, D. & D. Sperber. 1992. On verbal irony. *Lingua* 87: 53–76.

2012. *Meaning and Relevance.* Cambridge: Cambridge University Press.

Yamanashi, M. 1998. Some issues in the treatment of irony and related tropes. In *Relevance Theory: Applications and Implications*, ed. R. Carston & S. Uchida, 271–82. Amsterdam: John Benjamins.

Yus, F. 2000. On reaching the intended ironic interpretation. *International Journal of Communication* 10(1–2): 27–78.

2016. *Humour and Relevance.* Amsterdam: John Benjamins.

2017. Incongruity-resolution cases in jokes. *Lingua*; available at http://dx .doi.org/10.1016/j.lingua.2017.02.002.

Zalecki, J. 1990. *Communicative Multivocality: A Study of Punning, Metaphor and Irony.* Kraków: Nakl. Uniwersytetu Jagiellonskiego.

Index

A Modest Proposal, 1, 12, 60, 74
acting, 72, 73, 81
Alazon, 6
allusional pretence theory, 84-86, 91, 94
Amante, David J., 31
Aristotle, 11, 138, 141
art, 9, 80
as if-theory, 33-38, 102, 120, 154
Asterios Polyp, 130
asymmetry issue, 48, 49, 60, 70, 71, 91-95, 98, 102
Attardo, Salvatore, 61, 106, 113, 124, 136
attitude, 7, 14, 17, 24, 25, 35, 38, 43, 44, 48, 50, 60, 68, 69, 75, 80, 88-105, 107, 111, 113, 114, 115, 118, 119, 122, 126, 130, 132, 133, 140, 143, 144
  dissociative attitude, 45, 46, 50, 55, 62, 71
Austin, John L., 31, 156

Banksy, 5
Barbe, Katharina, 134, 136
benefits of irony, 104, 111
bridge content, 37, 38, 97, 98, 100, 102, 154
Brown, Mary. *See* allusional pretence theory

Camp, Elisabeth, 128, 134
Carston, Robyn, 37, 124
Clark, Herbert. *See* pretence theory
clues, 50, 73, 107, 109, 110, 115, 116, 117, 118, 119, 123, 135, 154
  traditional clues, 112-14, 118
Colston, Herbert L., 124, 134

context, 13, 19, 20, 49, 54, 55, 56, 97, 98, 101, 102, 108, 109, 110, 116, 117
contradiction issue, 22, 26
conversational maxims, 19, 155,
  quality maxim, 19, 20, 27, 29, 32, 35, 57, 85, 120
cooperative principle, 19, 154
critical pragmatics, 33, 120, 154
Curcó, Carmen, 61-62, 139, 142
Currie, Gregory, 82-83

dance, 9
Dews, Shelly, 104, 105, 111, 138
dissociation, 57-59
dramatic irony, 6, 65, 78, 129
Dynel, Marta, 103, 128

echo, 44, 46, 54-57, 66, 83, 85, 109, 114, 117-18, 119, 123, 135,
  echoic attribution, 43, 88
  echoic interpretation, 43
  echoic mention, 43
  pretense versus echo, 73-79
  strong notion, 118, 123
echoic account, 25, 59, 65, 71, 84, 89, 91, 93, 97, 102, 113, 115, 120, 121, 132
echoic reminder theory, 59-61, 86, 91, 94, 102, 132
Eiron, 6
exploit (a maxim), 19, 21, 27, 154

fiction, 6, 73, 80
figurative meaning, 20, 39, 52, 88
flout (a maxim), 19, 20, 27, 28, 32, 57, 85, 120, 155
  irony with no flouting, 27-28, 29, 35
Fowler, Henry W., 67, 75, 78

164

Index

165

Garmendia, Joana, 33, 34, 36, 90, 93, 102
Gerrig, Richard. *See* pretence theory
Gibbs, Raymond W., 124, 134
Giora, Rachel, 38–39, 56, 61, 62
Glucksberg, Sam. *See* allusional pretence theory, echoic reminder theory
graded salience hypothesis, 39, 156
Grice, H. Paul, 14, 18–31, 34, 50, 65, 66, 71, 72, 74, 84, 88, 89, 91, 92, 102, 113, 115, 120

Happé, Francesca, 52
Haverkate, Henk, 31, 90, 91, 93, 102
Hobbes, Thomas, 138
humour, 10, 17, 113, 126, 138–45
  incongruity theories, 138
  superiority theories, 138, 143
hyperbole, 12, 20, 114, 116, 117, 123

implicature, 18, 26, 27, 38, 81, 97, 98, 155
  conventional implicature, 18
  conversational implicature, 18, 20
    generalized (GCI), 20
    particularized, 20
  strong and weak, 37, 102, 156
indirect negation, 39, 61
insincerity, 32, 72, 73, 85, 86
  pragmatic insincerity, 85,
  transparent insincerity, 32
irony of fate, 3, 78, *See also* situational irony

Kant, Immanuel, 142
Kierkegaard, Søren, 142,
Korta, Kepa, 13, 30, 33, 99, 154
Kreuz, Roger J. *See* echoic reminder theory
Kumon-Nakamura, Sachi. *See* allusional pretence theory

lies, 32, 34, 73

make as if to say, 22, 26, 34, 72, 88
make-believe, 72, 73, 80, 86, 122
McDonald, Sky, 128
means of expression. *See* clues
meiosis, 20
mention, 155, *See also* echoic mention
metaphor, 12, 20, 22, 52, 109, 112, 156

meta-representation, 52
mimicking, 50, 79, 80, 81, 86, 119
Morris, Mark, 9
motivating belief, 35, 36, 120
Muecke, Douglas, 124, 134
music, 9

Nunberg, Geoffrey, 10, 128

Obama, 2, 107, 108, 117,
Oedipus, 2, 6
one-stage view of irony, 47, 59, 65, 66,
  See also two-stage view of irony

parody, 9, 10, 76, 79, 114, 126
Perry, John, 13, 33, 154
persuasion, 11, 12, 13
Plato, 138
point of irony, 29, 30, 33, 37, 99, 102
politeness theory, 105, 111, 154
Pollyanna, 70, 94
positive irony, 48, 49, 50, 60, 61, 70, 91–95, 96, 97, 101, 102, 104, 105
pretence, 24, 50, 85, 88, 114, 118, 119, 123, 135
  pretence versus echo, 73–79
  strong use, 73, 123
  weak use, 72
pretence theory, 60, 65–79, 89, 91, 94, 102, 113, 115, 120, 122

Quintilian, 12

Recanati, François, 81,
relevance theory, 14, 42, 47, 53, 63, 155
  principle of relevance, 76, 155
resemblance, 43
rhetoric, 11, 13, 17
risks of irony, 30, 104, 105, 107–12, 134
romantic irony, 7
Romeo and Juliet, 6

sarcasm, 9, 11
satire, 2, 9, 10, 108
Schopenhauer, Arthur, 142
Searle, John R., 31, 32, 156
Shostakovich, Dmitri, 9
simile, 12
situational irony, 3–5, 129, *See also* irony of fate

Index

Socratic irony, 7
speech act, 82, 85, 154
  felicity condition, 85
  preparatory condition, 155
  sincerity condition, 31, 32, 33, 36, 156
speech act theory, 31–33, 36, 91, 155, 156
Sperber, Dan. *See* Echoic account
Swift, Jonathan, 1, 8, 12, 60, 74, 75,

target, 118, 130, 131, 137, 140, *See also*
  victim
The Big Bang Theory, 2, 7, 127,
The New Yorker, 2, 107, 108, 117
The Sixth Sense, 6
theory of mind, 52
tinge hypothesis, 104–5

tone of voice, 24, 50, 71, 79, 112, 114,
  123, 135,
Turkish gay parade, 1
two-stage view of irony, 38, 39, 47, 59,
  65, 66, *See also* one-stage view of
  irony

verbal irony, 129
victim, 67, 69, 78, 118, 119, 129, 130–33,
  156

Walton, Kendall, 73, 80, 129
Warhol, Andy, 9
Wearing, Catherine, 124
Wilson, Deirdre. *See* echoic account
Winner, Ellen, 104, 105, 111

Printed in the United States
By Bookmasters